ACTIVE DISCUSSION
For Intermediate Learners 1

MP3

Navigate through Various Topics!
Become a discussion expert by probing into a variety of topics.

Explore Diverse Perspectives Around the World!
Acquire the global edge by discussing cultural issues.

Practice Productive English!
Improve your speaking and writing skills through dynamic interactions.

CARROT HOUSE

Curriculum Map

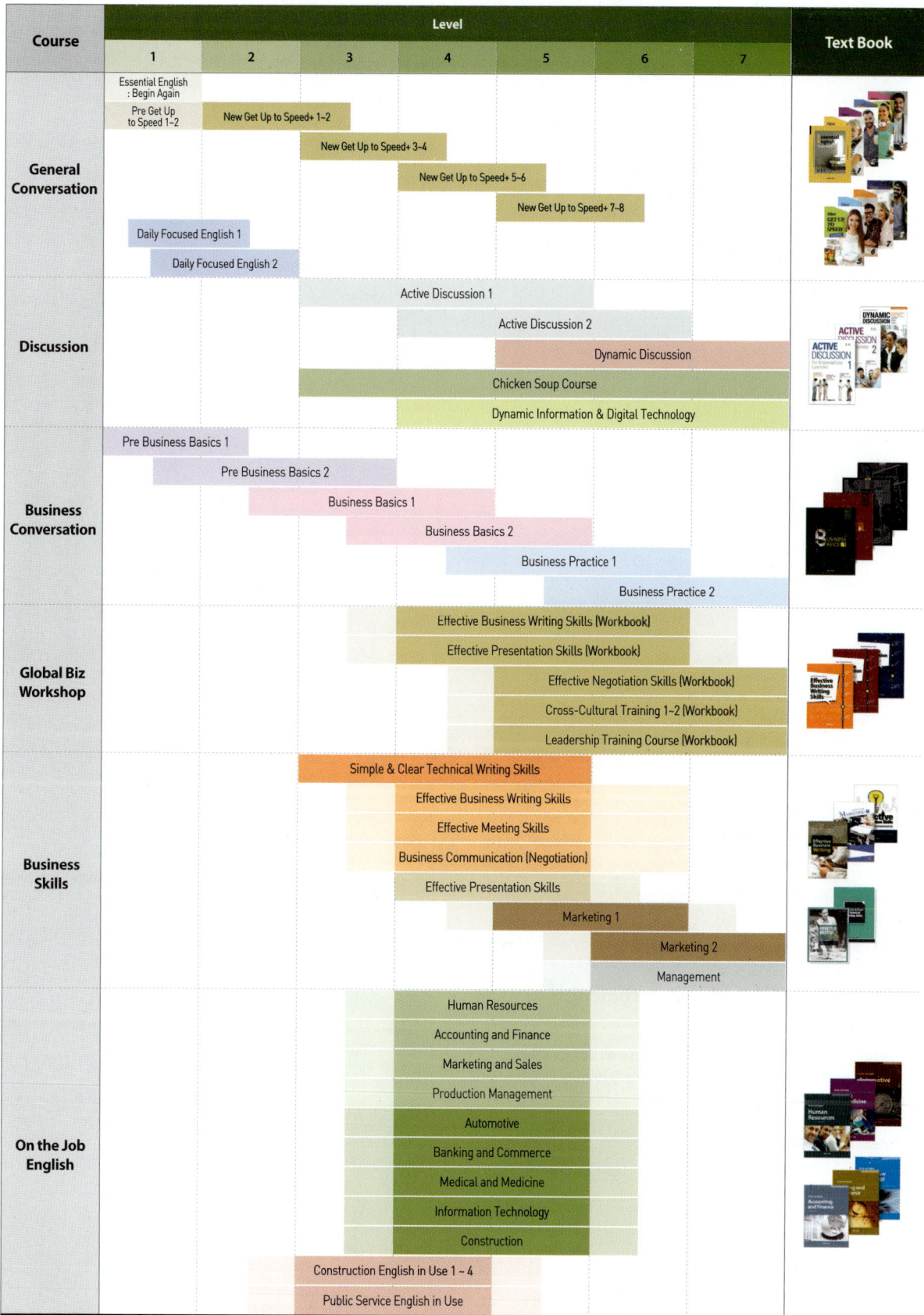

Course	Level 1	Level 2	Level 3	Level 4	Level 5	Level 6	Level 7
General Conversation	Essential English: Begin Again						
	Pre Get Up to Speed 1–2	New Get Up to Speed+ 1–2					
			New Get Up to Speed+ 3–4				
				New Get Up to Speed+ 5–6			
					New Get Up to Speed+ 7–8		
	Daily Focused English 1						
		Daily Focused English 2					
Discussion				Active Discussion 1			
				Active Discussion 2			
					Dynamic Discussion		
			Chicken Soup Course				
				Dynamic Information & Digital Technology			
Business Conversation	Pre Business Basics 1						
		Pre Business Basics 2					
		Business Basics 1					
			Business Basics 2				
				Business Practice 1			
					Business Practice 2		
Global Biz Workshop				Effective Business Writing Skills (Workbook)			
				Effective Presentation Skills (Workbook)			
					Effective Negotiation Skills (Workbook)		
					Cross-Cultural Training 1–2 (Workbook)		
					Leadership Training Course (Workbook)		
Business Skills				Simple & Clear Technical Writing Skills			
				Effective Business Writing Skills			
				Effective Meeting Skills			
				Business Communication (Negotiation)			
				Effective Presentation Skills			
					Marketing 1		
						Marketing 2	
						Management	
On the Job English					Human Resources		
					Accounting and Finance		
					Marketing and Sales		
					Production Management		
					Automotive		
					Banking and Commerce		
					Medical and Medicine		
					Information Technology		
					Construction		
			Construction English in Use 1 ~ 4				
			Public Service English in Use				

※ This Curriculum Map illustrates the entire line-up of textbooks at CARROT HOUSE.

CARROT HOUSE
P.O.Box #2924, St. Marys, Ontario, Canada

Active Discussion 1 For Intermediate Learners
© CARROT HOUSE

All rights reserved. No part of this publication may be reproduced, stored in a retrieval system, or transmitted in any form or by any means without the prior permission in writing of Carrot House.

Printed: April 2020

Author: Carrot Language Lab

ISBN 978-89-6732-033-1

Carrot Global Inc.
9F, 488, Gangnam St. , Gangnam-gu, Seoul, 06120, South Korea

Introduction »

Carrot House Methodology

Andragogical Approach & Productive English

The teaching of children (pedagogy) and adult learning (andragogy) are distinctively different. Pedagogy is akin to training and encourages convergent thinking and rote learning. It is compulsory, centered on the teacher and the imparting of information with minimal control by the learner. Andragogy, by contrast, is about education as freedom. It encourages divergent thinking and active learning. It is voluntary, learner-oriented and opens up vistas for continuing learning. Adults need to feel independent and in control of their learning. Therefore, Carrot House curriculum is based on andragogy and is designed to encourage learners' participation and engagement by providing more task-based activities and opportunities to frequently interact in the classroom.

People want to achieve communicative competence when they learn other languages. English education in EFL environments has been rather focused on the receptive skills of English—listening and reading—which simply increases learners' knowledge about a language, not the competence of using it. If people are well-equipped with productive skills—speaking and writing—they will be competent in English communication.

This is why Carrot House curriculum is designed to enhance learners' productive skills throughout the course. This andragogical approach of the Carrot House Curriculum, which focuses on productive English, will enable learners to achieve communication skills necessary for global competence. Carrot House's teaching philosophy and curriculum combine to provide a "Language for Success" for all learners.

Communicative Language Learning (CLL)

This communicative interaction, the essential component of language acquisition, does not occur in a typical, non-meaningful, fun-oriented conversation with native speakers. It occurs in a negotiated interaction through which a well-trained teacher provides the comprehensible input that is appropriate to the learners. The learners, at the same time, actively utilize the opportunities given to them by the teachers.

To this end, the Communicative Language Learning (CLL) method is employed in the field of Foreign Language Acquisition. The CLL method provides activities that are geared toward using language pragmatically, authentically and functionally with the intention of achieving meaningful purposes.

Course Overview

I. Objectives

 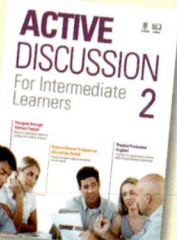 

The Active Discussion series is designed to improve learners' productive proficiency in English-speaking and to help learners give logical opinions on various subjects with confidence.
The books focus on a variety of different topics relating to daily life, current affairs, and culture.

This series will give students opportunities to enjoy presenting their ideas, while at the same time assimilating methods for developing strong opinions with confidence.

The Dynamic Discussion book, part of the discussion series, is designed for advanced learners in English.

II. Lesson Composition

This book consists of 5 Issues [12 lessons] based on topics of great interest to everyone including current affairs and culture. The composition of each lesson is as below.

■ Learning Objectives

·····> Learning objectives are provided at the beginning of each lesson to give specific learning goals. Precise learning objectives facilitate learners' ability to learn new skills. Check whether the objectives have been met at the completion of a lesson.

1 Warming Up! Voca-Space

·····> Diverse vocabulary from the two case articles is provided to learners. Learners, in small groups or pairs, define the meaning of the words on their own. These words are provided to prepare learners for the discussion.

2 Making a Case (Case A & Case B)

·····> This section covers a variety of debatable topics that provide learners with opportunities to discuss by expressing their own thoughts and opinions. Two case articles that may or may not be related are provided per lesson. By skimming through these articles, learners are provided with facts and ideas to develop their own opinions about various topics. Each article is followed by three activities that prepare the learners for the main discussion activity later in the lesson: **Stretch Your Thinking, Phrase Fit, and True or False?**

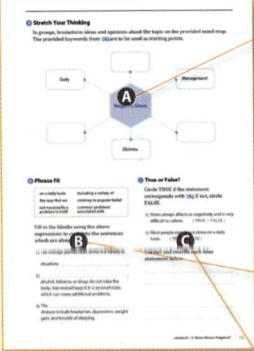

A Stretch Your Thinking

·····> Learners are presented with the main topic of the article and three key words that briefly summarize the article. Learners, in small groups or pairs, brainstorm ideas and opinions using the presented key words as starting points on a given topic. Learners are given opportunities to test their comprehension of the article as well as discuss the given topic using keywords from the article.

B Phrase Fit

·····> Learners practice article-related useful discussion expressions through completing sentences that briefly summarize the article.

C True or False?

·····> Learners are presented with two sentences about the article that are either true or false. Learners circle the word **True** when the statement is true and vice versa. Learners also correct the false statements by rewriting the sentences in the space provided. This activity will help learners check their understanding of the issues presented in the case articles.

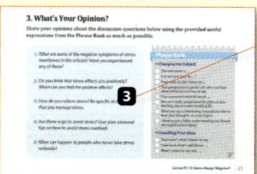

3. What's Your Opinion?

······▷ Learners share their opinions with others by responding to the discussion questions. Also, learners are provided with a checklist of useful expressions-Phrase Bank, which they will practice using during their discussions. The phrases that have not been checked (i.e. are unused) should be induced to be used in discussions. These useful expressions for discussions will facilitate learners' ability to form opinions and discuss differing topics in various situations.

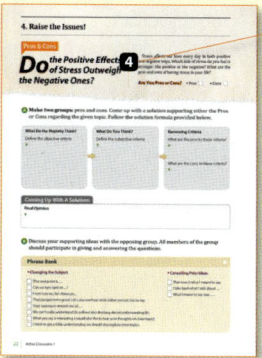

4. Raise the Issues!

······▷ For this main discussion activity, learners are provided with a statement which encourages discussions by actively expressing their opinions. A group of learners is divided into two subgroups, pro and con. This activity can also be done in pairs. Each subgroup develops their opinions in order to persuade the opposing subgroup. The subgroups also have to consider the other side of their opinion by asking and responding to questions. Learners are provided with a step-by-step formula to organize their opinions with supporting ideas.

Also, the checklist of useful discussion phrases- Phrase Bank is provided to help learners incorporate useful expressions in their discussions. Learners should utilize the vocabulary and expressions learned in the lessons during this debate. Through this activity, learners are able to form logical opinions as well as develop the ability to inquire about the other side of the debate.

5. Fun Forum

······▷ Learners are provided with interesting and fun discussion topics which they discuss in small groups. This activity is designed for students to enjoy discussions.

6. A Sneak Peek!

······▷ Learners pretend that they are a host to a Roundtable Discussion TV show. They are asked to give three questions regarding a topic in the next lesson. This activity prepares the learners for the upcoming lesson and focuses their interest on the topic.

III. Wrap Up

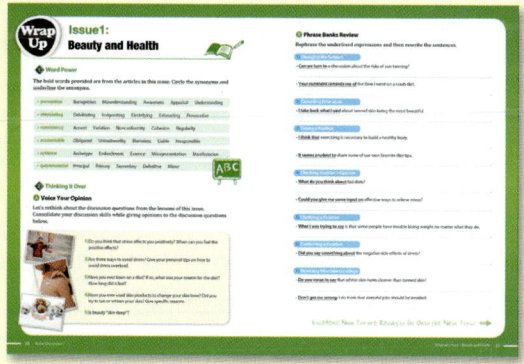

This book consists of five Wrap Up sections. The Wrap Up sections are based on the lessons for the five main issues. They will encourage the learners to develop discussion skills by providing opportunities to practice learned vocabulary and phrases.

Contents »

1 Beauty and Health

Topic	Giving Opinions	Phrase Bank	Fun Forum	Page Number
1. Is Stress Always Negative?	*To give logical opinions about stress and its side effects. Case A. The Downside of Stress Case B. The Upside of Stress	*** Changing the Subject** - The next point is…. - Can we turn (get) to…? - From now on, let's focus on…. - That perspective is good. Let's also see/hear what (other person) has to say. - Your comment reminds me of…. - We can't really understand (A) without also thinking about/ understanding (B). - What you say is interesting. I would also like to hear your thoughts on (new topic). - I think to get a fuller understanding we should also explore (new topic). *** Cancelling Prior Ideas** - That wasn't what I meant to say. - I take back what I said about…. - What I meant to say was….	**[Show & Tell]** What do you feel is the most valuable object you are carrying right now?	18
2. Is Your Diet Working?	*To give logical opinions about dieting and exercising. Case A. The Dieter's Dilemma Case B. Eat and Exercise!	*** Taking a Position** - I think that…. - I believe that…. - In my opinion,…. - My position is…. - It seems prudent to…. - Looking at all the options, it is best to…. - I feel compelled to…. - The reality is that…. *** Checking Another's Opinion** - What do you think about…? - What's your feeling on the issue of…? - Could you give me some input on…? - What's your take on…?	**[Every Cloud has a Silver Lining]** What has been the most life-changing experience you have ever had?	24
3. Culture Lab Tanned Skin vs White Skin, Which is More Beautiful?	*To give logical opinions about the perception of beauty and skin tone in terms of cultural differences. Case A. White Skin, The Asian Ideal Case B. Baking for Beauty: Tanning in Western Countries	*** Clarifying a Position** - What I meant was…. - What I was trying to say…. - Well, I think the answer is…. - Because…. *** Confirming a Position** - Did you say something about…? - Are you actually saying that…? - You mentioned to me that…. - …is that right? *** Resolving Misunderstandings** - Do you mean to say…? - I didn't mean it quite that way. - I'm sorry. I think you misunderstood what I meant. - Don't get me wrong.	**[Beauty and the Beast]** What is your perception of beauty?	30
Wrap Up: Issue 1 Beauty and Health		*** Word Power** - Antonyms & Synonyms *** Thinking it Over** - Voice Your Opinion, Phrase Banks Review		36

2 Daily Lives

Topic	Giving Opinions	Phrase Bank	Fun Forum	Page Number
4. Perfumes and Why We Love Them	*To give logical opinions about why perfume is so popular. Case A. Perfumes and Increased Sexual Attraction? Case B. Pleasing Scents and Self-Identification	*** Introducing Your Experience** - Let me tell you about one of my experiences…. - Let me tell you about one of my worst experiences…. - One of my best experiences was when…. - One of my worst experiences was when…. - I remember when…. - There was this time I was…. *** Beginning the Discussion** - Let's talk about…. - Let's discuss…. - It's a good idea to begin with…. - Should we begin with…?	**[Earthlings V]** What would you take on Earthling V?	38
5. Culture Lab Fermented Food: Cheese or Fermented Soybeans?	*To give logical opinions about fermented food in different cultures. Case A. The Spread of Cheese Culture Case B. Indigenous Asian Cuisine, Fermented Soybeans	*** Contributing Ideas** - How about…? - Maybe we could…. - What about this…? - To reach our goal, we could try…. - To get a range of ideas, why don't we…? - Thinking inside the box could lead us to…. - Thinking outside the box could lead us to…. - To challenge conventions, let's assume…. - Switching gears, let's consider the issue from a new angle. - Let's brainstorm first and judge later. *** Encouraging Ideas** - Brilliant! / I like that! / Awesome! / Good thinking! *** Expanding on Ideas** - That gives me an idea. - Another idea would be…. - Yeah, we could also….	**[Armchair Traveler]** What are your travel experiences? Have you experienced culture shock?	44
Wrap Up: **Issue 2 Daily Lives**		*** Word Power** - Antonyms & Synonyms *** Thinking it Over** - Voice Your Opinion, Phrase Banks Review		50

3 Ethics

Topic	Giving Opinions	Phrase Bank	Fun Forum	Page Number
6. Food Crisis	*To give logical opinions about global food crisis and actions to combat worldwide famine. Case A. The Global Food Crisis Case B. A Need for Global Effort to Combat Famine	*** Interrupting** - I'm sorry to cut you off, but…. - I'm sorry to interrupt, but…. - Excuse me for interrupting, but…. - Let's not discuss (topic) any further. - Let's break off our discussion. *** Disagreeing with Positions** - That certainly is one possibility, but…. - I'm not so sure about that because…. - That might be true, but…. - A lot of people might agree with that, but….	**[Fate or Free Will?]** Do you believe in fate or free will?	52

	Topic	Giving Opinions	Phrase Bank	Fun Forum	Page Number
7. Culture Lab Beautiful Comradeships		* To give logical opinions about organ donations and related cultural factors. Case A. Donating Life Case B. Culture of Organ Donations	* **Defending Positions** - Let me put it another way…. - I think the point I'm trying to make here is…. - Well, if you could just spare me a moment,…. - Understanding the idea requires deliberation. - To elucidate the idea,…. - The crux of the issue is…. * **Agreeing with Positions** - I'd have to agree that…. - I think that's a good point. - Sure/Right/Certainly/Absolutely/Exactly - That's all right. - What you're saying may be right. - It sounds good.	**[Good Deeds]** If you could choose to devote your life to a single cause, what would it be?	58
Wrap-Up: Issue 3 Ethics			* **Word Power** - Antonyms & Synonyms * **Thinking it Over** - Voice Your Opinion, Phrase Banks Review		64

4 Social Lives

	Topic	Giving Opinions	Phrase Bank	Fun Forum	Page Number
8. Expiration Date on Love?		* To give logical opinions about love and how to sustain a soul-mate relationship. Case A. The Science of Love Case B. Forever and Always: How-To's on Keeping a Soul-mate Relationship	* **Suggesting Options** - Would this be okay? - Would this work? - Would this fit our criteria? - What if we did this? * **Rejecting Options** - I don't think that would work because…. - We don't see eye to eye on…. - I don't share your view on…. * **Asking to Reconsider** - Why don't you think it over? - Please reconsider. - Could you think further about that? - Don't jump to conclusions.	**[Apple of My Eye]** What factors are important in choosing a partner?	66
9. Cyber Relationships		* To give logical opinions about online relationships. Case A. Online Connections Case B. Missing Out on Real Relationships	* **Looking for Assumptions** - We are assuming that…. - Is it really necessary that…? - Do we really have to…? - What would happen if we…? * **Recognizing Errors** - I apologize for my mistake. It's my fault. * **Accepting Options** - That would work! - That might be good! - That's a possibility! - That sounds quite convincing to me. - It sounds right to….	**[Captivating People]** Who was the most interesting person you have ever met?	72
10. Culture Lab Collectivism and Individualism in Dining		* To give logical opinions about cultural differences in dining in terms of group dining versus one-person dining.	* **Restating the Options** - This one has…. - The advantage of this option is…. - The disadvantage of this one is…. - To highlight/emphasize what has been said so far,…. - To expand upon the points made so far,….	**[Stranger than Food]** What is the strangest food you have ever eaten?	78

Topic	Giving Opinions	Phrase Bank	Fun Forum	Page Number
Case A. Eating Alone is Embarrassing? Case B. Tips for Solo Diners		*** Offering a Similar Instance or Expression** - In other words,…. - That is (to say)…. - …, so to speak,…. *** Pointing Out Mistakes** - I'm afraid it was off topic. - I don't think you have it quite right. - It's unreasonable to say….		
Wrap-Up: **Issue 4 Social Lives**		*** Word Power** - Antonyms & Synonyms *** Thinking it Over** - Voice Your Opinion, Phrase Banks Review		84

5 Our Earth

Topic	Giving Opinions	Phrase Bank	Fun Forum	Page Number
11. Global Warming: Let's Love Our Earth!	*** To give logical opinions about global warming and actions to combat it.** Case A. Earth is Heating Up Case B. The Bright Future of Alternative Energy	*** Prioritizing Criteria** - What is more important to you, (A) or (B)? - What do you value more? - Which is the least important? - How do you judge the worthiness of…? - Which factor is most relevant? - What aspect is most overlooked? - Weighing the options, it seems…. - The pros and cons dictate…. - Every issue has plusses and minuses. *** Stating Values** - To me, (A) is more important than (B). - To me, that doesn't matter. - To me, that is really important. - What we should really focus on is…. - Let's not get distracted by…. - It is easy to miss…. - In the long run, we should care most about…. - Over time, what will become apparent is….	**[Off the Record]** If you could omit one event in your life, what would it be?	86
12. Culture Lab Food Waste and Food Mileage	*** To give logical opinions about food waste and food mileage.** Case A. Wasteful Societies Case B. From Farm to Plate: How Far Did Your Dinner Travel?	*** Grasping the Meaning** - (Excuse me, but) what does (expression) mean? - What do you mean by…? - I'm sorry, but I didn't get what you said. - If we draw a conclusion,…. - If we connect the dots, then…. - Putting two and two together, we can see that…. *** Concluding** - In retrospect, this seems to…. - After considering all the main points,…. - Taking everything we've discussed into account,…. - On that note, we'll end by saying…. - All these points lead to…. - Thus, the overarching point is…. - In conclusion, the core point is….	**[Food You Can't Live Without]** If you had to choose only three foods and two drinks for the rest of your life, what would they be?	92
Wrap-Up: **Issue 5 Our Earth**		*** Word Power** - Antonyms & Synonyms *** Thinking it Over** - Voice Your Opinion, Phrase Banks Review		98

Answer Key 100

Situational & Useful Expressions for Discussion

Objective Expressions

◆ Beginning the Discussion
- Let's talk about….
- Let's discuss….
- It's a good idea to begin with….
- Should we begin with…?

◆ Changing the Subject
- The next point is….
- Can we turn/get to…?
- From now on, let's focus on….
- That perspective is good. Let's also see/hear what (other person) has to say.
- Your comment reminds me of….
- We can't really understand (A) without also thinking about/understanding (B).
- What you say is interesting. I would also like to hear your thoughts on (new topic).
- I think to get a fuller understanding we should also explore (new topic).

◆ Asking to Continue
- Please go on.
- Please go ahead.
- You've clearly thought about this topic. What else have you considered?
- Does what you say relate to…?
- What you say is (interesting, etc.). What else do you see/think?
- Your ideas sound great. Please tell me more.

◆ Referring to Material
- Please take a look at… for reference.
- Please consult….
- As you can see illustrated here,….
- Mapping the data gives us this picture.
- If we put all this data together, the picture is clear that….
- The best way to see my point is to look at….

◆ Expressing an Objective Viewpoint
- Objectively speaking,….
- Please think of (topic) objectively.
- Considering just the facts, it is clear that….
- Scientifically speaking, the case is….
- If we take a look at the big picture, it is clear that….
- In my culture, it's different. We like to….

◆ Summarizing
- In summary
- In short,….
- To reiterate my main point,….
- So, looking at everything together, it is clear that (main point).
- So, the basis of all that I said is that….

◆ Concluding
- In retrospect, this seems to….
- After considering all the main points,….
- Taking everything we've discussed into account,….
- On that note, we'll end by saying….
- All these points lead to….
- Thus, the overarching point is….
- In conclusion, the core point is….

Subjective Feelings, Opinions, and Judgments

◆ Introducing Your Experience
- Let me tell you about one of my experiences….
- Let me tell you about one of my worst experiences….
- One of my best experiences was when….
- One of my worst experiences was when….
- I remember when….
- There was this time I was….

◆ Expressing a Subjective Viewpoint

- Subjectively speaking,….
- The way I see it,….
- I think (opinion) is too subjective.
- In my mind,….

◆ Expressing Feelings

- I have a feeling that….
- What's your feeling on…?
- My feeling is that….
- What's your impression of…?

◆ Communicating Ideas Clearly

- What I'm really saying is that….
- What I mean is that….
- The premise of my thinking is….
- The root of my idea is….
- What it all boils down to is…
- To condense what I am saying, the main point is….

◆ Giving Another Opinion

- Besides,….
- In addition,….
- I have something to add to this.
- Likewise, it is also crucial to consider….
- Moreover, it is essential to see….
- To add yet another point,….
- In order to achieve balance, we must consider….

◆ Contributing Ideas

- How about…?
- Maybe we could….
- What about this…?
- To reach our goal, we could try….
- To get a range of ideas, why don't we…?
- Thinking inside the box could lead us to….
- Thinking outside the box could lead us to….
- To challenge conventions, let's assume….
- Switching gears, let's consider the issue from a new angle.
- Let's brainstorm first and judge later.

◆ Taking a Position

- I think that….
- I believe that….
- In my opinion,….
- My position is….
- It seems prudent to….
- Looking at all the options, it is best to….
- I feel compelled to….
- The reality is that….

◆ Voicing an Objection

- I'm against….
- I object to….
- I'm opposed to….
- I'm not in favor of….
- I have a different opinion about….

◆ Defending Positions

- Let me put it another way….
- I think the point I'm trying to make here is….
- Well, if you could just spare me a moment,….
- Understanding the idea requires deliberation.
- To elucidate the idea,….
- The crux of the issue is….

◆ Making Remarks

- In my opinion/view,….
- From my point of view,….
- As I see it….
- As far as I can tell,….
- To get to the core,….
- To finalize the debate,….

◆ Prioritizing Criteria

- What is more important to you, (A) or (B)?
- What do you value more?
- Which is the least important?

Situational & Useful Expressions for Discussion

- How do you judge the worthiness of…?
- Which factor is most relevant?
- What aspect is most overlooked?
- Weighing the options, it seems….
- The pros and cons dictate….
- Every issue has plusses and minuses.

◆ Stating Values

- To me, (A) is more important than (B).
- To me, that doesn't matter.
- To me, that is really important.
- What we should really focus on is….
- Let's not get distracted by….
- It is easy to miss….
- In the long run, we should care most about….
- Over time, what will become apparent is….

◆ Offering Judgment

- In my own judgment, (A) is right/wrong.
- Judging from….
- I'll leave it to your judgment.
- To cut to the chase,….
- Don't be too rash to judge.

◆ Offering a Guess or Inference

- I guess….
- It's just a guess, but I infer….
- It seems to me that….
- It seems only logical to assume….

◆ Attempting Persuasion

- Please hear me out on this.
- In my view, it is more….
- You might find it better to….
- To strike the right chord, we need to….
- My solution is a win-win situation.

Comprehension, Questions, and Misunderstandings

◆ Checking Another's Opinion

- What do you think about…?
- What's your feeling on the issue of…?
- Could you give me some input on…?
- What's your take on…?

◆ Asking Another's Viewpoint

- Is that all right?
- Can we discuss this?
- Do you have any objection?
- Would you agree?
- Is it right?

◆ Resolving Misunderstandings

- Do you mean to say…?
- I didn't mean it quite that way.
- I'm sorry. I think you misunderstood what I meant.
- Don't get me wrong.

◆ Understanding

- I see what you mean.
- I see your point.
- I can catch/grasp the point of what you're saying.

◆ Expressing Difficulty in Understanding

- (It) is difficult to understand.
- (It) is hard to make out.
- Your question/answer is vague.
- I think your statement is ambiguous.

◈ Addressing a Lack of Explanation
- I think it needs further explanation.
- That's not enough.
- It's still beyond my understanding.
- That doesn't make sense to me.

◈ Clarifying a Position
- What I meant was….
- What I was trying to say….
- Well, I think the answer is….
- Because….

◈ Restating the Options
- This one has….
- The advantages of this option are….
- The disadvantage of this one is….
- To highlight/emphasize what has been said so far,….
- To expand upon the points spoken so far,….

◈ Looking for Assumptions
- We are assuming that….
- Is it really necessary that…?
- Do we really have to…?
- What would happen if we…?

◈ Asking for More Time
- Let's think about it.
- How about giving it a little more thought?
- Could you give me more time to think about it?

◈ Asking for Repetition
- Excuse me?
- Pardon me?
- Would you repeat that, please?
- Could you speak up, please?
- I didn't catch what you said.

◈ Offering a Similar Instance or Expression
- In other words,….
- That is (to say)….
- …, so to speak,….

◈ Grasping the Meaning
- (Excuse me, but) what does (expression) mean?
- What do you mean by…?
- I'm sorry, but I didn't get what you said.
- If we draw a conclusion,….
- If we connect the dots, then….
- Putting two and two together, we can see that….

◈ Grasping the Intention
- Please get straight to the point.
- Let me know what's on your mind.
- Let's be open with each other.
- Please tell me what you really think.

Positive Comments and Remarks

◈ Encouraging Ideas
- Brilliant!
- I like that!
- Awesome!
- Good thinking!

◈ Expanding on Ideas
- That gives me an idea.
- Another idea would be….
- Yeah, we could also….

◈ Agreeing with Positions
- I'd have to agree that….
- I think that's a good point.
- Sure/Right/Certainly/Absolutely/Exactly
- That's all right.

Situational & Useful Expressions for Discussion

- What you're saying may be right.
- It sounds good.

◆ **Expressing Partial Agreement**

- I agree with you to some extent, but….
- Your point of view is all right, but….

◆ **Accepting Options**

- That would work!
- That might be good!
- That's a possibility!
- That sounds quite convincing to me.
- It sounds right to….

◆ **Expressing Affirmative (Positive) Agreement**

- You said it!
- I think so.
- You're right.
- I agree with you on that point.
- I assent to your idea.
- Oh, I agree entirely.
- That's exactly what I'm saying.

Negative Comments and Remarks

◆ **Cancelling Prior Ideas**

- That wasn't what I meant to say.
- I take back what I said about….
- What I meant to say was….

◆ **Rejecting Options**

- I don't think that would work because….
- We don't see eye to eye on….
- I don't share your view on….

◆ **Disagreeing with Positions**

- That certainly is one possibility, but….

- I'm not so sure about that because….
- That might be true, but….
- A lot of people might agree with that, but….

◆ **Pointing Out Mistakes**

- I'm afraid it was off topic.
- I don't think you have it quite right.
- It's unreasonable to say….

◆ **Interrupting**

- I'm sorry to cut you off, but….
- I'm sorry to interrupt, but….
- Excuse me for interrupting, but….
- Let's not discuss (topic) any further.
- Let's break off our discussion.

Politeness, Courtesy, and Requests

◆ **Suggesting Options**

- Would this be okay?
- Would this work?
- Would this fit our criteria?
- What if we did this?

◆ **Making Additional Remarks**

- Could I add something?
- There is one more thing to say.
- Just one more thing….

◆ **Giving an Uncertain Answer**

- That's a tough question for me.
- I'm afraid I can't answer that right now.
- I really don't have an answer.
- I'll find out.
- I don't know.

◆ **Confirming a Position**

- Did you say something about…?

- Are you actually saying that…?
- You mentioned to me that….
- …is that right?

◆ Recognizing Errors

- I apologize for my mistake.
- It's my fault.

◆ Asking to Reconsider

- Why don't you think it over?
- Please reconsider.
- Could you think further about that?
- Don't jump to conclusions.

◆ Expressing Consideration

- I'll think about….
- Let me think about….
- If possible,….
- I need some time to think about….

◆ Reserving an Answer

- I'm afraid I can't say yes at the moment.
- I can't say anything now.
- I'm sorry, but I haven't decided yet.
- I'll let you know later.
- I have nothing further to say.

◆ Asking for Another Occasion

- Would you give me another chance?
- Please let me try again.
- Let's make it some other time.

◆ Addressing Sarcastic Remarks

- Don't make light of this.
- This is serious….
- I don't mean to be funny, but….

◆ Asking for Restraint

- Please, no more argument.
- Can I make a point?
- Please listen to what I have to say.
- I would like to interject something.

◆ Rejecting Restraint

- But this really is of no concern to you.
- Wait! Let me finish (what I'm saying).

◆ Dismissing a Minor Matter

- It doesn't matter.
- It isn't a matter of importance.
- It's a small thing.

Miscellaneous

◆ Soothing Mental Excitement

- Please calm down.
- Don't be upset.
- Take it easy.
- There's no need to get excited.

LESSON 01

Is Stress Always Negative?

Learning Objectives

After completing this lesson, you will be able to…

- Give logical opinions about stress and its side effects.
- Utilize useful discussion phrases regarding changing the subject and cancelling prior ideas.

1. Warming Up!

A *Check* the words you know and *circle* the words that you do not yet know.

Voca-space

self-medicate	react	supposedly
distress	unrelieved	manifest
perception	eustress	self-improvement
immune system	Alzheimer's	stimulating
equipped	insomnia	adrenaline
utilizing		

B In groups, help each other to find the meaning of the circled words. The dictionary should be the last resort!

2. Making a Case [A]

Read the article below. Gather ideas about the topic as you read the article.

The Downside of Stress

Stress is something that the average person comes into contact with **on a daily basis.** We experience stress as we **react** to changes in our environment. Due to stress's commonplace nature, our bodies are **equipped** with resources to cope with it. Stress is **not necessarily a problem in itself**, but it can have negative effects when it goes **unrelieved** for too long.

When stress cannot be relieved, it can lead to **distress**, a negative stress reaction. An estimated 43 percent of adults suffer from health problems related to distress. The symptoms of distress can **manifest** themselves in different ways, **including a variety of** physical, mental, and emotional issues. Some of the most **common problems associated with** distress are headaches, high blood pressure, depression, weight gain, and **insomnia**.

The way that we deal with stress affects how strongly we feel its negative effects. Practicing good stress **management** techniques can help minimize the negative effects. Stress is most harmful when people try to **self-medicate** using alcohol, tobacco, or drugs. **Contrary to popular belief**, these **supposedly** relaxing substances tend to keep the body in a stressed state and only cause more problems.

18 | Active Discussion 1

A Stretch Your Thinking

In groups, brainstorm ideas and opinions about the topic on the provided mind map. The provided keywords from [A] are to be used as starting points.

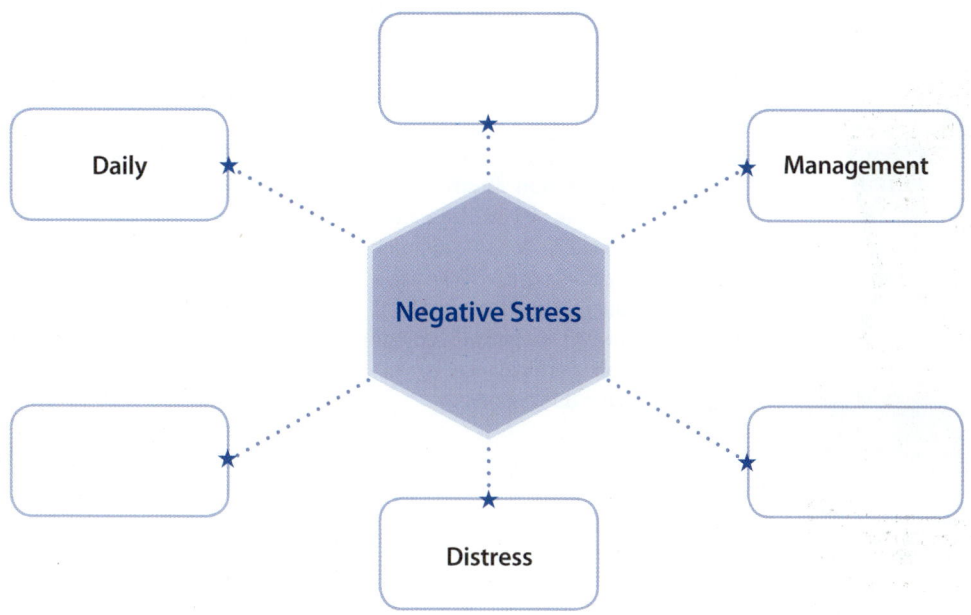

B Phrase Fit

on a daily basis	including a variety of
the way that we	contrary to popular belief
not necessarily a problem in itself	common problems associated with

Fill in the blanks using the above expressions to complete the sentences which are about [A].

1) The average person faces stress in a variety of situations _____.

2) _____, alcohol, tobacco, or drugs do not relax the body, but instead keep it in a stressed state, which can cause additional problems.

3) The _____ distress include headaches, depression, weight gain, and trouble of sleeping.

C True or False?

Circle TRUE if the statement corresponds with [A]; if not, circle FALSE.

1) Stress always affects us negatively and is very difficult to relieve.   (TRUE / FALSE)

2) Most people experience stress on a daily basis.   (TRUE / FALSE)

Correct and rewrite each false statement below.

_____

_____

_____

_____

2. Making a Case [B]

Read the article below. Gather ideas about the topic as you read the article.

The Upside of Stress

Many people have a very negative **perception** of stress, but stress is not all bad. Recent research proves that a reasonable amount of stress can affect us positively. Positive stress, also known as **eustress**, can help motivate us toward **self-improvement** and **improve job performance** by encouraging us to get things done.

Stress causes the release of hormones, such as **adrenaline**, which have very positive effects **in small amounts**. These hormones give us the **burst of energy** necessary to get things done. **Some research suggests** these hormones have a positive effect on the **immune system** and can even protect against diseases like **Alzheimer's** by **stimulating** brain function.

Everyone needs some stress in their life in order to feel challenged and satisfied. It is when this stress becomes **too much to handle** that the negative side effects **come into play**. The trick to successfully **utilizing** stress to your benefit is not to try to eliminate it, but to try to manage the negative symptoms.

A Stretch Your Thinking

In groups, brainstorm ideas and opinions about the topic on the provided mind map. The provided keywords from [B] are to be used as starting points.

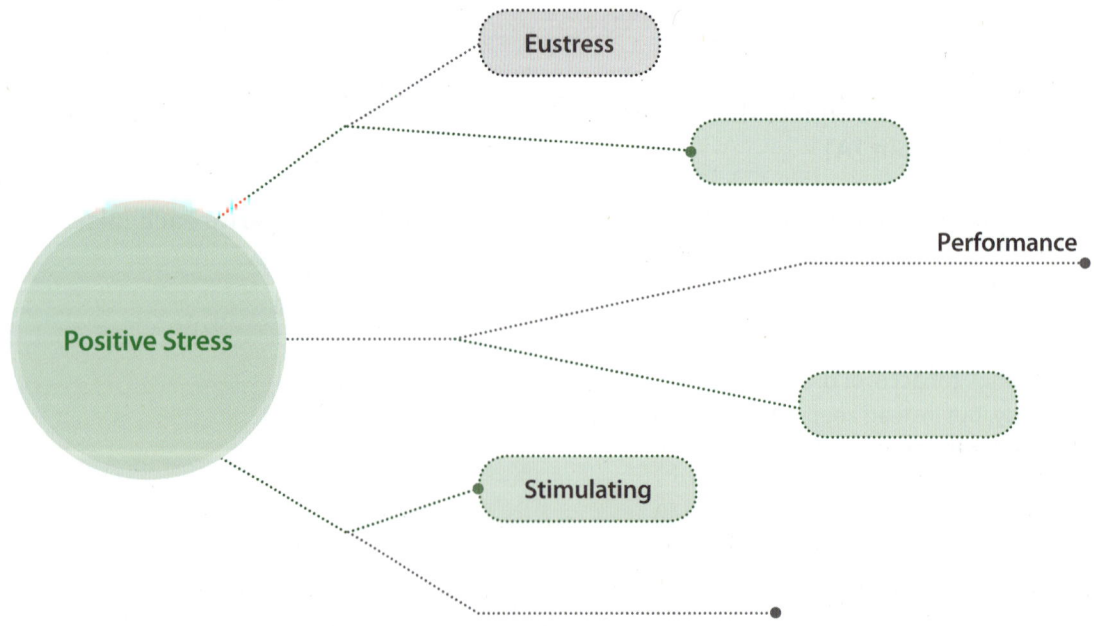

B Phrase Fit

in small amounts	too much to handle
improve job performance	burst of energy
some research suggests	come into play

Fill in the blanks using the above expressions to complete the sentences which are about [B].

1) _____ that stress can improve the immune system and help protect against Alzheimer's by challenging our brains.

2) The negative side effects of stress only _____ when stress becomes unmanageable.

3) Stress causes the release of hormones, such as adrenaline, to give us the _____ _____ we need to accomplish a task.

C True or False?

Circle TRUE if the statement corresponds with [B]; if not, circle FALSE.

1) Eustress can provide us with the motivation that we need to get things done.
(TRUE / FALSE)

2) Stress always damages the brain, causing diseases such as Alzheimer's.
(TRUE / FALSE)

Correct and rewrite each false statement below.

_____
_____
_____
_____

3. What's Your Opinion?

Share your opinions about the discussion questions below using the provided useful expressions from the Phrase Bank as much as possible.

1) What are some of the negative symptoms of stress mentioned in the articles? Have you experienced any of these?

2) Do you think that stress affects you positively? When can you feel the positive effects?

3) How do you relieve stress? Be specific in the ways that you manage stress.

4) Are there ways to avoid stress? Give your personal tips on how to avoid stress overload.

5) What can happen to people who never take stress seriously?

Phrase Bank

• Changing the Subject
- ☐ The next point is….
- ☐ Can we turn (get) to…?
- ☐ From now on, let's focus on….
- ☐ That perspective is good. Let's also see/hear what (other person) has to say.
- ☐ Your comment reminds me of….
- ☐ We can't really understand (A) without also thinking about/understanding (B).
- ☐ What you say is interesting. I would also like to hear your thoughts on (new topic).
- ☐ I think to get a fuller understanding we should also explore (new topic).

• Cancelling Prior Ideas
- ☐ That wasn't what I meant to say.
- ☐ I take back what I said about….
- ☐ What I meant to say was….

4. Raise the Issues!

Pros & Cons

Do the Positive Effects of Stress Outweigh the Negative Ones?

Stress affects our lives every day in both positive and negative ways. Which side of stress do you feel is stronger: the positive or the negative? What are the pros and cons of having stress in your life?

Are You Pros or Cons?   • Pro ☐   • Con ☐

A Make two groups: pros and cons. Come up with a supporting argument for your position on the given topic. Follow the reasoning method provided below.

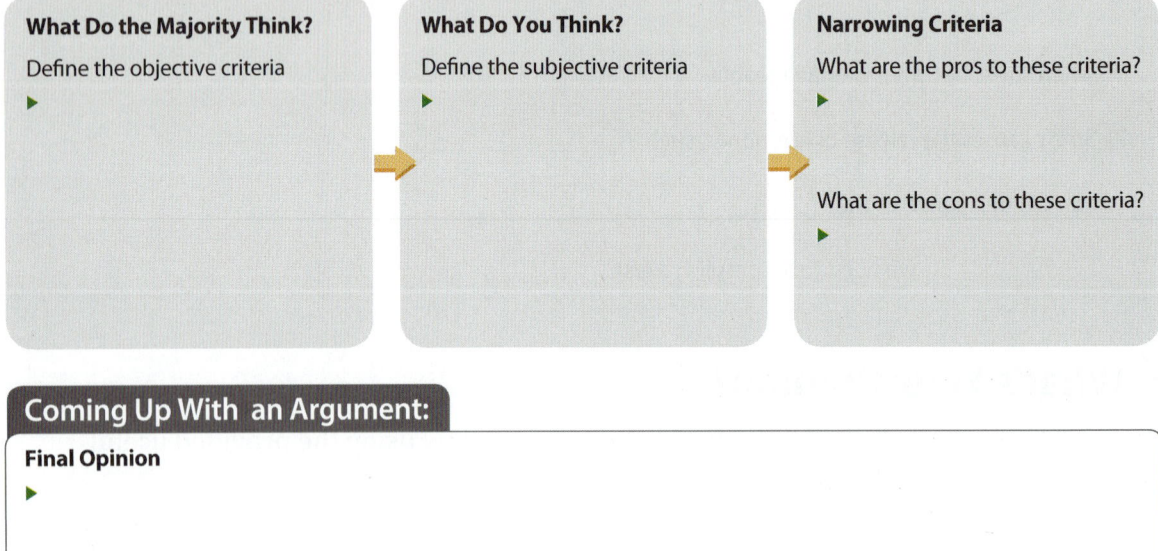

What Do the Majority Think?	What Do You Think?	Narrowing Criteria
Define the objective criteria ▶	Define the subjective criteria ▶	What are the pros to these criteria? ▶ What are the cons to these criteria? ▶

Coming Up With an Argument:

Final Opinion
▶

B Discuss your supporting ideas with the opposing group. All members of the group should participate in giving and answering the questions.

Phrase Bank

• **Changing the Subject**
- ☐ The next point is….
- ☐ Can we turn (get) to…?
- ☐ From now on, let's focus on….
- ☐ That perspective is good. Let's also see/hear what (other person) has to say.
- ☐ Your comment reminds me of….
- ☐ We can't really understand (A) without also thinking about/understanding (B).
- ☐ What you say is interesting. I would also like to hear your thoughts on (new topic).
- ☐ I think to get a fuller understanding we should also explore (new topic).

• **Cancelling Prior Ideas**
- ☐ That wasn't what I meant to say.
- ☐ I take back what I said about….
- ☐ What I meant to say was….

Active Discussion 1

5. Fun Forum

Show & Tell

Q: What do you feel is the most valuable object you are carrying right now? Hide the object and give hints so that your group can guess what the object is. The members in your group get 3 guesses. Ready, set, go!

List of 3 Questions

1	2	3

A Sneak Peek!

If you were a host to a Roundtable Discussion program, what would you ask about the following topic? Write three questions and discuss about it.

[Is Your Diet Working?]

1.
2.
3.

02 LESSON

Is Your Diet Working?

- **Learning Objectives**

  After completing this lesson, you will be able to…

- Give logical opinions about dieting and exercising.
- Utilize useful discussion phrases regarding taking a position and checking another's opinion.

1. Warming Up!

A *Check* the words you know and *circle* the words that you do not yet know.

Voca-space

accountable	routine	dilemma
metabolism	appropriate	consistency
physiology	boosting	pleasant
determines	excess	
cookie-cutter approaches		

B In groups, help each other to find the meaning of the circled words. The dictionary should be the last resort!

2. Making a Case [A]

Read the article below. Gather ideas about the topic as you read the article.

The Dieter's Dilemma

Anyone who has ever dieted knows that losing weight isn't always easy. You might follow your diet and exercise plan **to a T**, but still fail to see the scale budge at the end of the day. How can you seemingly **be doing everything right**, but still not lose a pound? This is a **dilemma** which affects dieters the world over.

There are several factors that contribute heavily to dieting success and failure. One common problem is **strictly adhering to fad diets** that do not take into consideration your unique **physiology** and **metabolism**. These diets' **cookie-cutter approaches** to weight loss may not be **appropriate** for you. For long-term success, it's essential to find **a routine that works for** your body.

Lack of **consistency** is one of the biggest diet-killers. You might go on a diet for a while, then quit before you have made any measurable progress. For this reason, it is helpful to have a dieting buddy to be **accountable** to. You and your partner can motivate each other to continue. **Most importantly**, to achieve success you must continue to think positively and keep going until your **end goal is in sight**.

Active Discussion 1

A Stretch Your Thinking

In groups, brainstorm ideas and opinions about the topic on the provided mind map. The provided keywords from [A] are to be used as starting points.

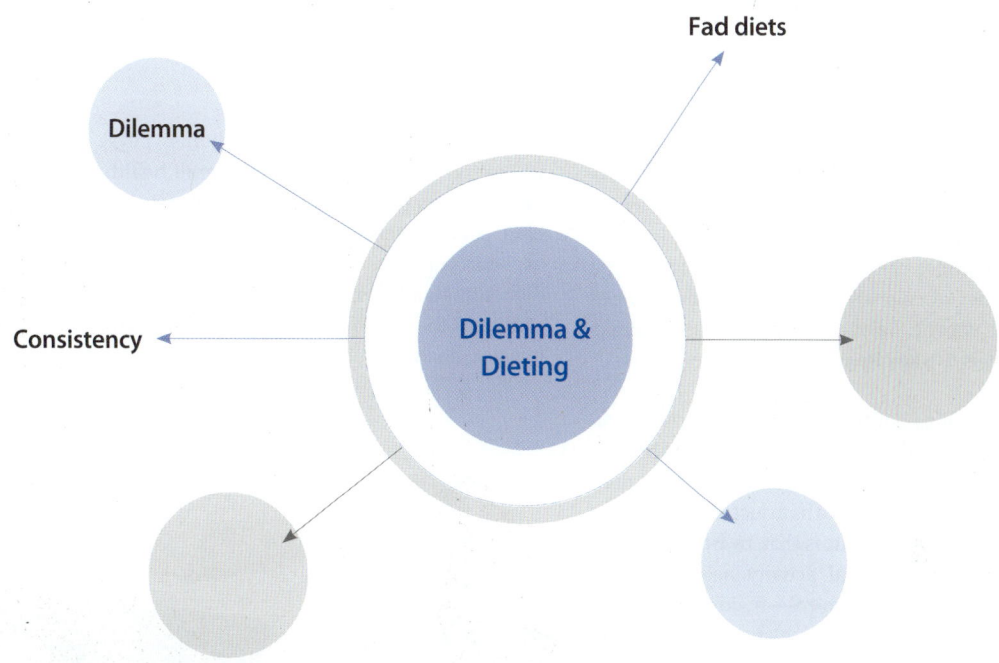

B Phrase Fit

to a T	be doing everything right
strictly adhering to	most importantly
end goal is in sight	a routine that works for

Fill in the blanks using the above expressions to complete the sentences which are about [A].

1) One reason for failure is .... diet plans that are not designed for your body's needs.

2) Even though you are following the diet plan ...., the scale is just not moving the way you want it to.

3) ...., the key to dieting success is to keep thinking positively and never giving up.

C True or False?

Circle TRUE if the statement corresponds with [A]; if not, circle FALSE.

1) A dieting buddy can help you maintain motivation to continue your diet.
(TRUE / FALSE)

2) Fad diets provide a good, well-tested way to achieve your dieting goals.
(TRUE / FALSE)

Correct and rewrite each false statement below.

....

....

....

....

Lesson 02 / Is Your Diet Working? 25

2. Making a Case [B]

Read the article below. Gather ideas about the topic as you read the article.

Eat and Exercise!

Regular exercise can have a big impact on **the overall success of** your weight loss plan. To understand how this works, **it's helpful to think of** weight loss as simple math. The number of calories that you eat minus the number of calories that you burn **determines** your weight. Balancing these numbers effectively **is the key to guaranteeing** weight loss.

As well as burning off **excess** calories, regular exercise also helps boost your **metabolism**. For this reason, combining exercise with dieting is more effective than just dieting **on its own. An added bonus** is that, by **boosting** your metabolism, physical activity helps you lose weight while eating more—making your overall weight loss experience speedier and more **pleasant**.

In addition to accelerating weight loss, physical exercise can improve your overall **health**. Research has proven that regular exercise can help prevent serious health problems, such as heart disease, stroke, hypertension, and diabetes. Making exercise **a part of your daily routine** is the key to long-term weight loss and physical health.

A Stretch Your Thinking

In groups, brainstorm ideas and opinions about the topic on the provided mind map. The provided keywords from [B] are to be used as starting points.

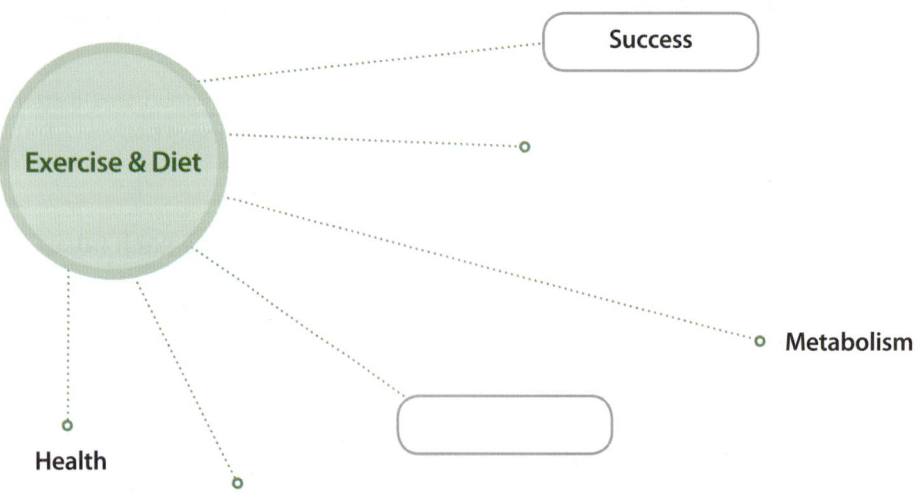

B Phrase Fit

the overall success of	on its own
it's helpful to think of	an added bonus
is the key to guaranteeing	a part of your daily routine

Fill in the blanks using the above expressions to complete the sentences which are about **[B]**.

1) Combining diet with exercise _____ that your diet is a success.

2) An effective exercise plan can help determine _____ your fitness regimen.

3) Physical activity in combination with a diet can yield better results than simply dieting _____.

C True or False?

Circle TRUE if the statement corresponds with **[B]**; if not, circle FALSE.

1) A healthy diet is the most important factor in achieving weight loss.
(TRUE / FALSE)

2) Exercising daily is the key to short-term weight loss and physical health.
(TRUE / FALSE)

Correct and rewrite each false statement below.

_____

_____

_____

_____

3. What's Your Opinion?

Share your opinions about the discussion questions below using the provided useful expressions from the Phrase Bank as much as possible.

1) Have you ever been on a diet? If so, what was your reason for the diet? How long did it last?

2) What are some fad diets that you know? Do you know anyone who has lost weight with them?

3) How important do you think exercise is to staying healthy? Give specific reasons.

4) Which types of physical activity do you enjoy? What is your current fitness routine? Do you think it is effective?

5) Do people in your country eat a well-balanced diet?

Phrase Bank

• Taking a Position
- ☐ I think that….
- ☐ I believe that….
- ☐ In my opinion,….
- ☐ My position is….
- ☐ It seems prudent to….
- ☐ Looking at all the options, it is best to….
- ☐ I feel compelled to….
- ☐ The reality is that….

• Checking Another's Opinion
- ☐ What do you think about…?
- ☐ What's your feeling on the issue of…?
- ☐ Could you give me some input on…?
- ☐ What's your take on…?

4. Raise the Issues!

Pros & Cons

Is Looking Good More Important than Feeling Good?

A good diet and regular exercise have a variety of benefits, including weight loss and improving health. Why should you change your fitness routine? Is losing weight to look good a better motivation than improving your health condition to feel good?

Are You Pros or Cons?   • Pro ☐   • Con ☐

A Make two groups: pros and cons. Come up with a supporting argument for your position on the given topic. Follow the reasoning method provided below.

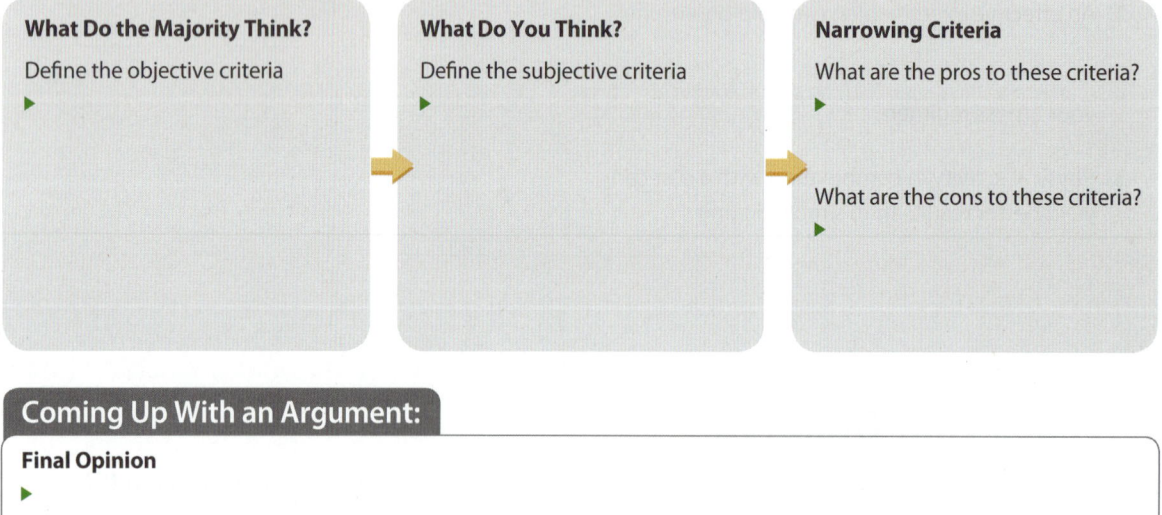

What Do the Majority Think?
Define the objective criteria
▸

What Do You Think?
Define the subjective criteria
▸

Narrowing Criteria
What are the pros to these criteria?
▸

What are the cons to these criteria?
▸

Coming Up With an Argument:

Final Opinion
▸

B Discuss your supporting ideas with the opposing group. All members of the group should participate in giving and answering the questions.

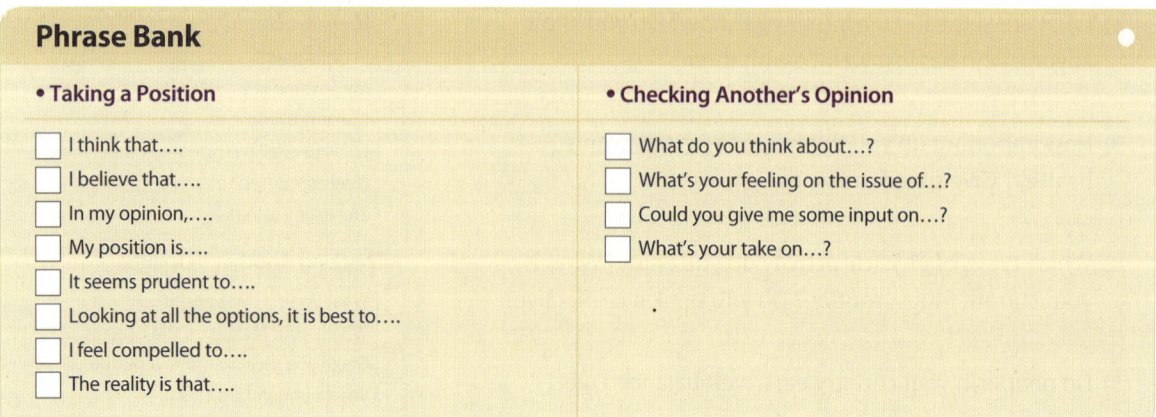

Phrase Bank

• **Taking a Position**
☐ I think that….
☐ I believe that….
☐ In my opinion,….
☐ My position is….
☐ It seems prudent to….
☐ Looking at all the options, it is best to….
☐ I feel compelled to….
☐ The reality is that….

• **Checking Another's Opinion**
☐ What do you think about…?
☐ What's your feeling on the issue of…?
☐ Could you give me some input on…?
☐ What's your take on…?

5. Fun Forum

Every Cloud has a Silver Lining

Q1 What has been the most life-changing experience you've ever had? Be specific and give reasons why when discussing it with your group. Also, write down other members' life-changing experiences.

Q2 Now choose one life-changing experience your group member had that you would like to experience. Explain to your group the reason behind your choice.

A Sneak Peek!

If you were a host to a Roundtable Discussion program, what would you ask about the following topic? Write three questions and discuss about it.

[Tanned versus White Skin, Which is More Beautiful?]

1.
2.
3.

03 ★ Culture Lab

Tanned Skin vs White Skin, Which is More Beautiful?

Learning Objectives
After completing this lesson, you will be able to…

- Give logical opinions about the perception of beauty and skin tone in terms of cultural differences.
- Utilize useful discussion phrases regarding clarifying a position, confirming a position, and resolving misunderstandings.

1. Warming Up!

A *Check* the words you know and *circle* the words that you do not yet know.

Voca-space

fair	pigments	publicity
epitome	inventions	mainstream
melanin	status symbol	innocent
prescribed	quintessential	complexion
high-end	exposure	

B In groups, help each other to find the meaning of the circled words. The dictionary should be the last resort!

2. Making a Case [A]

Read the article below. Gather ideas about the topic as you read the article.

White Skin, The Asian Ideal

In countries across Asia, **fair** skin is often viewed as the **epitome** of beauty. This view has caused skin-whitening to become a huge industry in countries like Taiwan, where an estimated 50 percent of women **shell out big cash** to lighten their skin tone. The Asian skin-whitening market is valued at over $18 billion. The products have become so **mainstream** that even **high-end** Western cosmetic brands, such as Chanel and Christian Dior, **are putting out** Asia-exclusive whitening lines.

Skin whitening **typically involves** using chemicals to try to lighten or even out the **complexion** by lessening the amount of **melanin** in the skin. Many whitening treatments come **with a hefty price tag** and can be found in a variety of forms, including lotions, pills, injections, and even laser treatments.

Despite their seemingly **innocent** promises, these pigment-reducing treatments are **not without their risks**. By removing **pigments** like melanin from the skin, the treatments reduce your body's natural protection against the sun's rays. This **increases the likelihood of** skin damage and skin cancer. Despite the dangers, whitening products and treatments have found a firm place in the Asian beauty market.

A Stretch Your Thinking

In groups, brainstorm ideas and opinions about the topic on the provided mind map. The provided keywords from [A] are to be used as starting points.

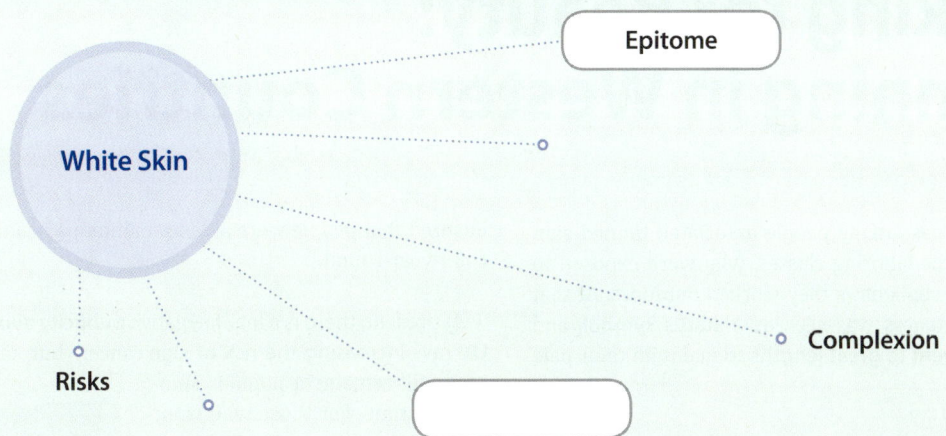

Culture Lab

B Phrase Fit

shell out big cash	are putting out
not without their risks	typically involves
with a hefty price tag	increases the likelihood of

Fill in the blanks using the above expressions to complete the sentences which are about [A].

1) The skin-whitening industry has found success in countries across Asia, where an increasingly large number of people are willing to _____ for whiter skin.

2) The industry has become so popular that even Western luxury cosmetic brands, such as Chanel and Christian Dior, _____ their own high-end whitening lines.

3) Many of these treatments come _____ and are available in many different forms, such as injections and laser treatments.

C True or False?

Circle TRUE if the statement corresponds with [A]; if not, circle FALSE.

1) Skin lightening is healthy because it prevents exposure to the sun's harmful rays.
(TRUE / FALSE)

2) Skin whitening treatments usually use chemicals to lighten the complexion by reducing the amount of melanin in the skin.
(TRUE / FALSE)

Correct and rewrite each false statement below.

....
....
....
....
....
....

Lesson 03 / Tanned Skin vs White Skin, Which is More Beautiful? | 31

2. Making a Case [B]

Read the article below. Gather ideas about the topic as you read the article.

Baking for Beauty:
Tanning in Western Countries

In the past, many people associated tanned skin with the laboring classes, who were exposed to harsh sunlight as they worked outdoors. At that time, whiteness was seen as a **status symbol**, and women **went to great lengths to** maintain their pale skin.

This all started to change at the turn of the twentieth century when doctors began to acknowledge the **health benefits** of sun **exposure**. It was a popularly **prescribed** treatment for a variety of illnesses, including fatigue and Vitamin D deficiency. At this time, sun bathing became associated with good health and **gained popularity among** the wealthy. **In the decades that followed, inventions** such as tanning beds ensured that people were able to maintain a healthy color year-round.

At present, there is a lot of negative **publicity** about **UV rays increasing the risk of** skin cancer, but tanning still remains a popular summer pastime. For those who want to avoid the risks of UV rays, there are a variety of "fake and bake" options, including spray tans and sunless tanning creams. **However you accomplish it**, a sun tan remains a **quintessential** summer accessory in many Western countries.

A Stretch Your Thinking

In groups, brainstorm ideas and opinions about the topic on the provided mind map. The provided keywords from [B] are to be used as starting points.

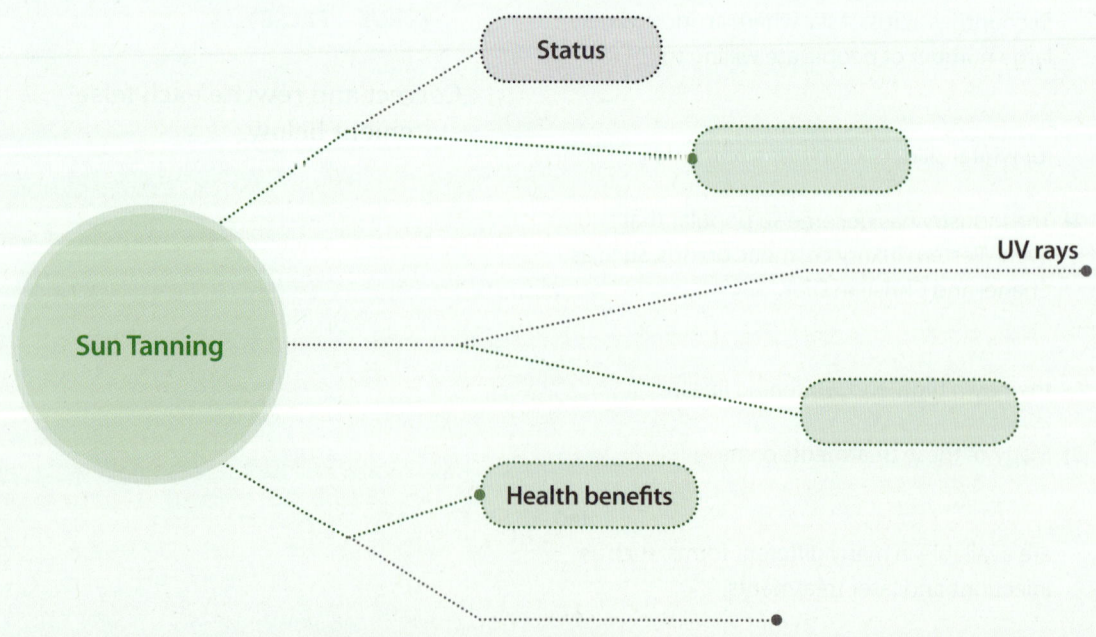

B Phrase Fit

gained popularity among	increasing the risk of
went to great lengths to	this all started to change
however you accomplish it	in the decades that followed

Fill in the blanks using the above expressions to complete the sentences which are about **[B]**.

1) In the past, many women _____ _____ maintain their pale skin due to the status symbol of whiteness.

2) Before the negative publicity about UV rays, sun bathing was considered healthy and _____ _____ the wealthy.

3) _____ , a tan is still regarded as a summer essential in many Western cultures.

C True or False?

Circle TRUE if the statement corresponds with **[B]**; if not, circle FALSE.

1) Recently, many doctors have started prescribing tanning as a medical treatment.
(TRUE / FALSE)

2) Despite the health risks, many people still enjoy sun tanning in Western countries.
(TRUE / FALSE)

Correct and rewrite each false statement below.

3. What's Your Opinion?

Share your opinions about the discussion questions below using the provided useful expressions from the Phrase Bank as much as possible.

1 Have you ever tried to suntan? How did you feel about your appearance after?

2 Have you ever used skin products to change your skin tone? Did you try to tan or whiten your skin? Share your thoughts in detail.

3 In your country, do people prefer white or dark skin? Why do you think this is the case?

4 Are you concerned about the health risks of sun exposure? What are some ways to protect your skin from the sun's harmful rays?

5 Is beauty "skin deep"?

Phrase Bank

• **Clarifying a Position**
☐ What I meant was….
☐ What I was trying to say….
☐ Well, I think the answer is….
☐ Because….

• **Confirming a Position**
☐ Did you say something about…?
☐ Are you actually saying that…?
☐ You mentioned to me that….
☐ …is that right?

• **Resolving Misunderstandings**
☐ Do you mean to say…?
☐ I didn't mean it quite that way.
☐ I'm sorry. I think you misunderstood what I meant.
☐ Don't get me wrong.

4. Raise the Issues!

Pros & Cons

Is White Skin More Attractive Than Tan Skin?

Skin whitening and tanning both have health risks associated with them, but people around the world continue to pursue these beauty extremes. This is an area where cultural preference is strong. Can one skin color be considered better than others? Does white skin look better than tan skin?

Are You Pros or Cons?   • Pro ☐   • Con ☐

A Make two groups: pros and cons. Come up with a supporting argument for your position on the given topic. Follow the reasoning method provided below.

What Do the Majority Think?
Define the objective criteria
▶

What Do You Think?
Define the subjective criteria
▶

Narrowing Criteria
What are the pros to these criteria?
▶

What are the cons to these criteria?
▶

Coming Up With an Argument:

Final Opinion
▶

B Discuss your supporting ideas with the opposing group. All members of the group should participate in giving and answering the questions.

Phrase Bank

• Clarifying a Position
☐ What I meant was….
☐ What I was trying to say….
☐ Well, I think the answer is….
☐ Because….

• Confirming a Position
☐ Did you say something about…?
☐ Are you actually saying that…?
☐ You mentioned to me that….
☐ …is that right?

• Resolving Misunderstandings
☐ Do you mean to say…?
☐ I didn't mean it quite that way.
☐ I'm sorry. I think you misunderstood what I meant.
☐ Don't get me wrong.

5. Fun Forum

Beauty and the Beast

What is your perception of beauty? List five traits of a beautiful person below.

Q1

A beautiful person...

1.
2.
3.
4.
5.

Q2 **Now gather into groups of two or more. Compare your list of traits of a beautiful person with others. How are they different? How are they similar?**

_____
_____
_____
_____
_____

A Sneak Peek!

If you were a host to a Roundtable Discussion program, what would you ask about the following topic? Write three questions and discuss about it.

[Food Crisis in the World]

1.
2.
3.

Lesson 03 / Tanned Skin vs White Skin, Which is More Beautiful? | 35

Issue 1:
Beauty and Health

1 Word Power

The bold words provided are from the articles in this issue. Circle the synonyms and underline the antonyms.

• perception	Recognition	Misunderstanding	Awareness	Appraisal	Understanding
• stimulating	Debilitating	Invigorating	Electrifying	Exhausting	Provocative
• consistency	Accord	Variation	Nonconformity	Cohesion	Regularity
• accountable	Obligated	Untrustworthy	Blameless	Liable	Irresponsible
• epitome	Archetype	Embodiment	Essence	Misrepresentation	Manifestation
• quintessential	Principal	Primary	Secondary	Definitive	Minor

2 Thinking it Over

A Voice Your Opinion

Let's rethink about the discussion questions from the lessons of this issue. Consolidate your discussion skills while giving opinions to the discussion questions below.

1) Do you think that stress affects you positively? When can you feel the positive effects?

2) Are there ways to avoid stress? Give your personal tips on how to avoid stress overload.

3) Have you ever been on a diet? If so, what was your reason for the diet? How long did it last?

4) Have you ever used skin products to change your skin tone? Did you try to tan or whiten your skin? Give specific reasons.

5) Is beauty "skin deep"?

B Phrase Banks Review

Rephrase the underlined expressions and then rewrite the sentences.

1) Changing the Subject

- <u>Can we turn to</u> a discussion about the risks of sun tanning?

  ....

- <u>Your comment reminds me of</u> the time I went on a crash diet.

  ....

2) Cancelling Prior Ideas

- <u>I take back what I said</u> about tanned skin being the most beautiful.

  ....

3) Taking a Position

- <u>I think that</u> exercising is necessary to build a healthy body.

  ....

- <u>It seems prudent to</u> share some of our own favorite diet tips.

  ....

4) Checking Another's Opinion

- <u>What do you think about</u> fad diets?

  ....

- <u>Could you give me some input on</u> effective ways to relieve stress?

  ....

5) Clarifying a Position

- <u>What I was trying to say</u> is that some people have trouble losing weight no matter what they do.

  ....

6) Confirming a Position

- <u>Did you say something about</u> the negative side effects of stress?

  ....

7) Resolving Misunderstandings

- <u>Do you mean to say</u> that whiter skin looks cleaner than tanned skin?

  ....

- <u>Don't get me wrong</u>; I do think that stressful jobs should be avoided.

  ....

Excellent! Now You are Ready to Go Onto the Next Topic!

LESSON 04

Perfumes and Why We Love Them

- **Learning Objectives**

  After completing this lesson, you will be able to…

- Give logical opinions about why perfume is so popular.
- Utilize useful discussion phrases regarding introducing your experience and beginning a discussion.

1. Warming Up!

A *Check* the words you know and *circle* the words that you do not yet know.

Voca-space

dramatic	advanced	appealing	hormones
combine	scent	stimulate	day and age
fragrance	interest	attraction	appetite
pheromones	civilized	desire	attention
pronounced	vivid	triggered	

B In groups, help each other to find the meaning of the circled words. The dictionary should be the last resort!

2. Making a Case [A]

Read the article below. Gather ideas about the topic as you read the article.

Perfumes and Increased Sexual Attraction?

In any given year, 66% of men and 75% of women find themselves buying cologne or perfume. Researchers **believe that** part of the reason women love receiving perfume (and also why men love giving perfume as a gift) is **due to pheromones**. Pheromones are **hormones thought to stimulate** sexual **appetite** or **interest** and they are **triggered** by **scent**.

So, do women love perfume because it makes them want to have sex? No, actually the scent has a more **dramatic** effect upon men. While the effect is **less pronounced** in women, certain colognes worn by men have **been known to produce** a similar **desire** in women. Although a link between the scent of perfume and increased sexual desire has been found, researchers do not believe that it explains the desire to wear perfume on a daily basis.

In fact, **most scientists believe** that human pheromones and their impact upon our behavior have decreased over the years as we have become more **advanced** and **civilized**. While most scientists conclude that scent once played a rather large part in human mating habits, they believe that it has **relatively little to do with** sexual **attraction** in this **day and age**.

Thus, the love of perfume may be only partly instinctual. Then what can explain our love for perfumes? What are some of the possible underlying factors for this fad?

A Stretch Your Thinking

In groups, brainstorm ideas and opinions about the topic on the provided mind map. The provided keywords from [A] are to be used as starting points.

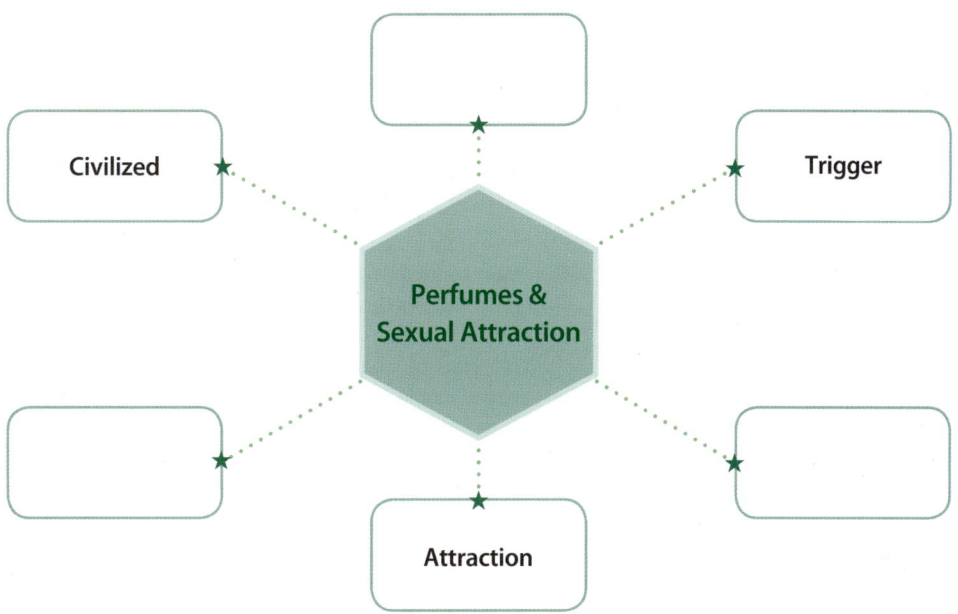

B Phrase Fit

thought to stimulate	believe that
relatively little to do with	due to
less pronounced	most scientists believe
been known to produce	

Fill in the blanks using the above expressions to complete the sentences which are about [A].

1) Pheromones are .... sexual interest via special scents.

2) While the effect is .... in women, certain colognes worn by men have .... a similar desire

3) Nowadays, ... that human pheromones and their impact upon our behavior have decreased.

C True or False?

Circle TRUE if the statement corresponds with [A]; if not, circle FALSE.

1) Some researchers believe that part of the reason men love giving perfume as a gift is due to pheromones. (TRUE / FALSE)

2) Most scientists believe that the impact of pheromones on human behavior has increased over the years due to advancements in modern society. (TRUE / FALSE)

Correct and rewrite each false statement below.

2. Making a Case [B]

Read the article below. Gather ideas about the topic as you read the article.

Pleasing Scents and Self-Identification

So, then why do women love perfume so much, and why is it such a popular gift during the holidays? It actually seems to be due to the simple feeling created by wearing any **fragrance** that one finds **appealing**.

Of course, it does **not really matter why** precisely a woman loves wearing perfume. All that is **truly important** is that she does love smelling great and the **attention** she receives when wearing her favorite perfume. In time, the perfume and the scent of her own body **will combine into** a singular aroma that **will literally become** her own scent.

As the sense of smell **can recall** the most **vivid** of memories, it is this unique scent of a woman combined with her perfume that people tend to remember most when thinking of that person. Men will often buy the same perfume for a woman even years after she has ceased using it because it is the scent they have come to identify with that woman.

Ⓐ Stretch Your Thinking

In groups, brainstorm ideas and opinions about the topic on the provided mind map. The provided keywords from [B] are to be used as starting points.

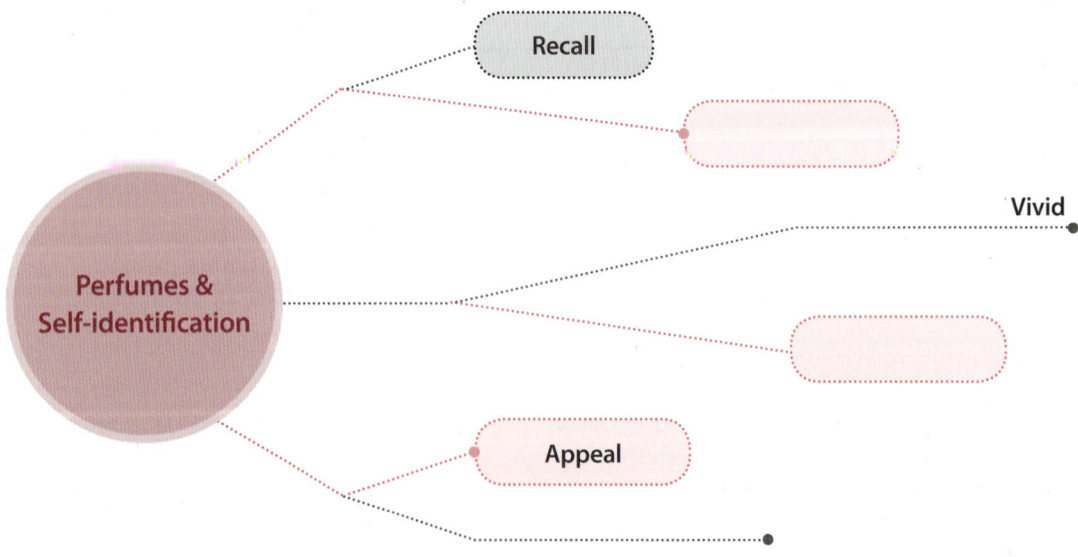

B Phrase Fit

> will literally become
> will combine into
> truly important
> not really matter why
> can recall

Fill in the blanks using the above expressions to complete the sentences which are about **[B]**.

1) It is often the case that the scent _____ _____ something that identifies the person that wears the perfume.

2) The sense of smell _____ vivid personal memories and images.

3) All that is _____ is that people love smelling great and the attention they receive when wearing their favorite perfume.

C True or False?

Circle TRUE if the statement corresponds with **[B]**; if not, circle FALSE.

1) In time, the perfume and the scent of the individual's body will combine into a singular aroma that will come to literally identify the person by scent. (TRUE / FALSE)

2) Our sense of smell and vivid images from our memories are often connected to each other. (TRUE / FALSE)

Correct and rewrite each false statement below.

_____

_____

_____

3. What's Your Opinion?

Share your opinions about the discussion questions below using the provided useful expressions from the Phrase Bank as much as possible.

1) What are pheromones and how do they relate to the wearing of perfume?

2) How important is wearing perfume to you, and what kind of scents do you like?

3) When do you use perfume, and what do you hope it will do for you or others?

4) Can you identify specific individual scents on women and men after they have worn the same cologne for a period of time?

5) What kind and how many different memories do perfume scents create for you?

Phrase Bank

• **Introducing Your Experience**
- ☐ Let me tell you about one of my experiences....
- ☐ Let me tell you about one of my worst experiences....
- ☐ One of my best experiences was when....
- ☐ One of my worst experiences was when....
- ☐ I remember when....
- ☐ There was this time I was....

• **Beginning the Discussion**
- ☐ Let's talk about....
- ☐ Let's discuss....
- ☐ It's a good idea to begin with....
- ☐ Should we begin with...?

4. Raise the Issues!

Pros & Cons

Wearing Perfume Increases Sexual Attraction?

The love of perfume by both men and women may be completely instinctual and somehow related to sexuality. However, the fact is that perfume just plain smells great and, therefore, 'spacing' puts us in a good mood. Who does not like something that smells good—be it a pot roast or a garden lily? Of course, pot roast has a tendency to make us hungry, so what does the smell of fine perfume make us? There has to be a really good reason why perfume is so popular now, right? Specifically, does wearing perfume increase sexual attraction?

Are You Pros or Cons? • Pro ☐ • Con ☐

A Make two groups: pros and cons. Come up with a supporting argument for your position on the given topic. Follow the reasoning method provided below.

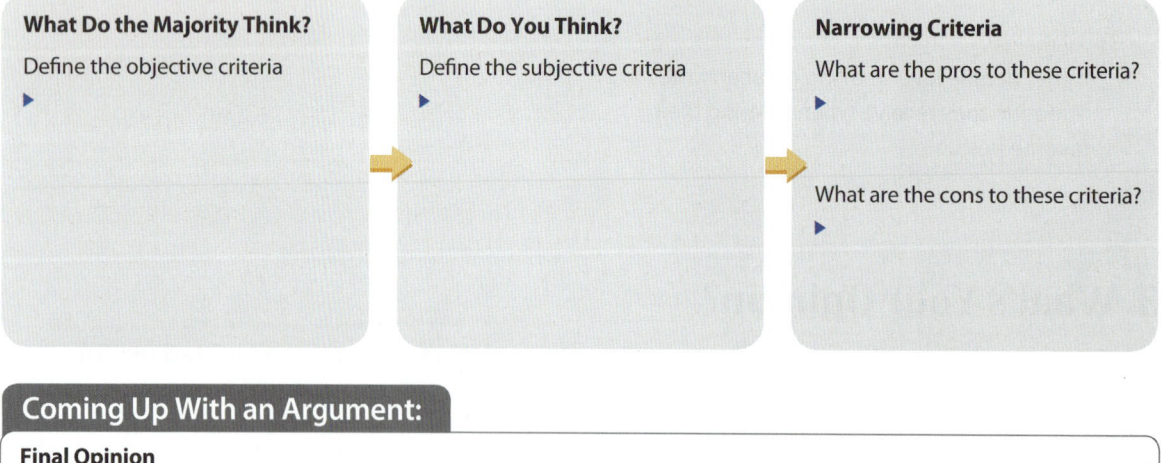

What Do the Majority Think?	What Do You Think?	Narrowing Criteria
Define the objective criteria	Define the subjective criteria	What are the pros to these criteria? ▶ What are the cons to these criteria? ▶

Coming Up With an Argument:

Final Opinion
▶

B Discuss your supporting ideas with the opposing group. All members of the group should participate in giving and answering the questions.

Phrase Bank

• Introducing Your Experience
- ☐ Let me tell you about one of my experiences…
- ☐ Let me tell you about one of my worst experiences…
- ☐ One of my best experiences was when…
- ☐ One of my worst experiences was when…
- ☐ I remember when…
- ☐ There was this time I was…

• Beginning the Discussion
- ☐ Let's talk about…
- ☐ Let's discuss…
- ☐ It's a good ideaa to begin with…
- ☐ Should we begin with…?

5. Fun Forum

EARTHLINGS V

Q1 Get into small groups and discuss items to put on board the spacecraft, **Earthlings V**. How many ideas can you think of? Make a list of specific items.

Ideas for Items to put on *Earthlings V*:

_____
_____
_____
_____

Q2 Now continue your discussion. Space and weight are very limited on the spacecraft. From your list, your group can select only 3 items to go on board. Which ones are they, and why?

Our Final 3 Items are

A Sneak Peek!

If you were a host to a Roundtable Discussion program, what would you ask about the following topic? Write three questions and discuss about it.

[The Best Fermented Food On Earth]

1. _____
2. _____
3. _____

Lesson 04 / Perfumes and Why We Love Them | 43

05 ★ Culture Lab

Fermented Food:
Cheese or Fermented Soybeans?

Learning Objectives
After completing this lesson, you will be able to…

- Give logical opinions about fermented food in different cultures.
- Utilize useful discussion phrases regarding contributing ideas, encouraging ideas, and expanding on ideas.

1. Warming Up!

A *Check* the words you know and *circle* the words that you do not yet know.

Voca-space

delicacy	predating	serendipitously
unique	indigenous	stumbled upon
dietary staple	essential	condiment
hearty	hype	longevity
embraced	pinpointing	purported
savory		

B In groups, help each other to find the meaning of the circled words. The dictionary should be the last resort!

2. Making a Case [A]

Read the article below. Gather ideas about the topic as you read the article.

The Spread of Cheese Culture

With origins **predating** recorded history, there is **no conclusive evidence pinpointing** exactly when and where the dairy-based **delicacy** first came into existence. Evidence of ancient cheese has been discovered across Europe and even in the royal tombs of ancient Egypt.

The cheese-making process **is believed to have been** discovered as early as 8,000 B.C. Legend has it that nomads storing milk in containers made of animal stomachs **serendipitously stumbled upon** the process. This is due to the fact that animal stomachs contain rennet, **a key ingredient in** the cheese fermentation process.

By the time the Roman Empire was well established, the Romans had developed cheese making into an art. While expanding their empire across Europe, Romans carried their cheese-making traditions to local peoples across the continent. All over Europe, many populations **embraced** cheese, eventually developing their own **unique** varieties and culture related to the product.

Over the centuries, cheese making has become **a firmly established part of** the European culture, with countries like the UK boasting an estimated 700 distinct local varieties of cheese and the average French citizen consuming 26.3 kilograms of the product on a yearly basis.

Although the true origins of cheese remain **shrouded in mystery**, this fermented food has spread across the globe to become a **dietary staple** in countries worldwide.

A Stretch Your Thinking

In groups, brainstorm ideas and opinions about the topic on the provided mind map. The provided keywords from [A] are to be used as starting points.

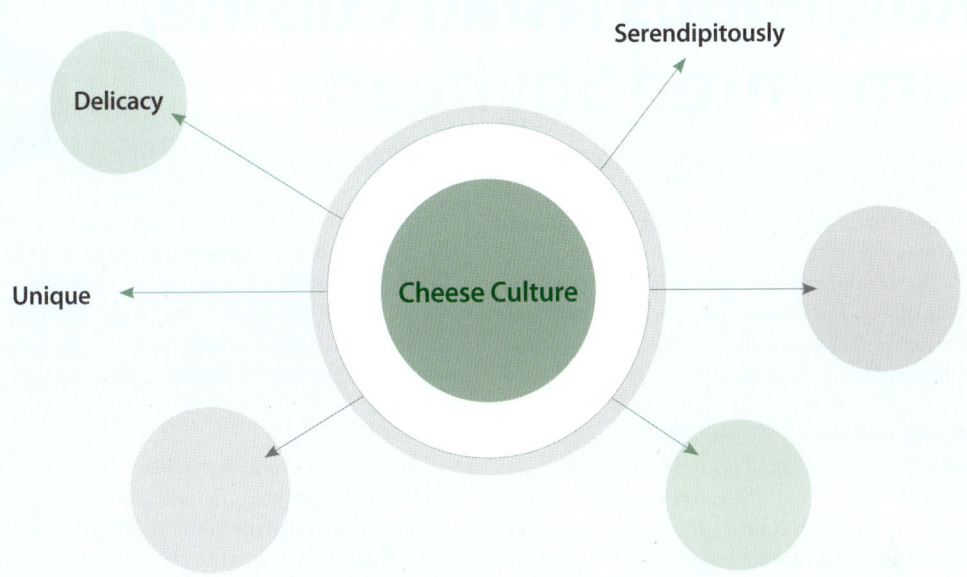

B Phrase Fit

no conclusive evidence	shrouded in mystery
is believed to have been	a key ingredient in
a firmly established part of	exactly when and where

Fill in the blanks using the above expressions to complete the sentences which are about [A].

1) Although cheese's roots remain _____, cheese has spread around the world to become a part of the food culture of many countries.

2) Animal stomachs contain rennet, _____ the cheese-making process.

3) The process of making cheese _____ discovered around 8,000 BC.

C True or False?

Circle TRUE if the statement corresponds with [A]; if not, circle FALSE.

1) Cheese is believed to have been first discovered by the ancient Egyptians.
(TRUE / FALSE)

2) Many countries in Europe have developed their own distinct varieties of cheese.
(TRUE / FALSE)

Correct and rewrite each false statement below.

_____

_____

_____

Lesson 05 / Fermented Food: Cheese or Fermented Soybeans? 45

2. Making a Case [B]

Read the article below. Gather ideas about the topic as you read the article.

Indigenous Asian Cuisine, Fermented Soybeans

Fermented soybeans are **an essential part of** many traditional Asian recipes. Historically, the **condiment** has been **relatively unknown outside of** Asia, but it is recently finding its way onto supermarket shelves worldwide due to its **purported** health **benefits** and **hearty** taste.

Manufactured **using an age-old process** in which dried soybeans are ground up and fermented for several months, fermented soybean requires no artificial additives for preservation. In addition, the super food **has been found to contain** many essential vitamins, minerals, and linoleic acid, a substance **believed to have the power to** prevent cancer. Fermented soybean paste is also rumored to be able to extend **longevity** and reduce body fat.

In addition to numerous health benefits, fermented soybean paste is an excellent complement to many foods. The **savory** paste can be eaten **in many forms** and does not lose any of its health benefits when cooked. It is commonly used as a base for soups and stir-fries, as well as in its raw form with vegetables and other foods.

For many reasons, fermented soybean paste is gaining popularity around the globe. Even if you do not believe all the **hype** about the health benefits, the taste alone is reason enough to try this traditional health food.

A Stretch Your Thinking

In groups, brainstorm ideas and opinions about the topic on the provided mind map. The provided keywords from [B] are to be used as starting points.

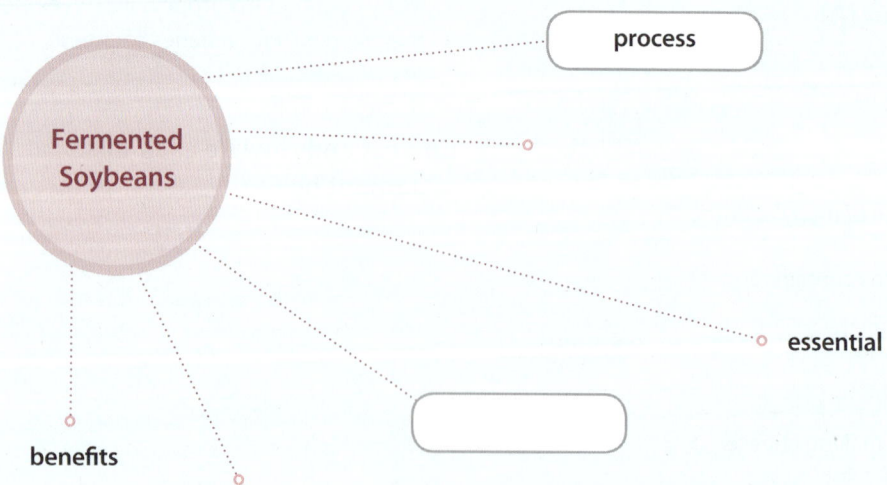

B Phrase Fit

an essential part of	using an age-old process
has been found to contain	in many forms
relatively unknown outside of	believed to have the power to

Fill in the blanks using the above expressions to complete the sentences which are about [B].

1) The savory fermented soybean paste can be eaten _____ and does not lose any of its health benefits when cooked.

2) The fermented soybean paste is useful in many dishes, making it _____ traditional Asian cuisine.

3) Although common in Asian cooking, the condiment was _____ Asia until recently.

C True or False?

Circle TRUE if the statement corresponds with [B]; if not, circle FALSE.

1) Fermented soybean paste is currently finding its way onto supermarket shelves worldwide due to its purported health benefits.
(TRUE / FALSE)

2) Fermented soybeans have many health benefits, including improving eyesight.
(TRUE / FALSE)

Correct and rewrite each false statement below.

....
....
....

3. What's Your Opinion?

Share your opinions about the discussion questions below using the provided useful expressions from the Phrase Bank as much as possible.

1) How do some people believe the first cheese was created?

2) What is your favorite kind of cheese? What sort of flavor does it have?

3) What are some of the purported health benefits of fermented soybeans? Do you believe they are true?

4) What are some other fermented foods that you know of?

5) How important is eating healthily to you? What types of food do you think should be included in a healthy diet?

Phrase Bank

• **Contributing Ideas**
☐ How about…?
☐ Maybe we could….
☐ What about this…?
☐ To reach our goal, we could try….
☐ To get a range of ideas, why don't we…?
☐ Thinking inside the box could lead us to….
☐ Thinking outside the box could lead us to….
☐ To challenge conventions, let's assume….
☐ Switching gears, let's consider the issue from a new angle.
☐ Let's brainstorm first and judge later.

• **Encouraging Ideas**
☐ Brilliant! / I like that! / Awesome! / Good thinking!

• **Expanding on Ideas**
☐ That gives me an idea.
☐ Another idea would be….
☐ Yeah, we could also….

4. Raise the Issues!

Pros & Cons

Are Fermented Foods Better In Their Original State?

Fermenting food is an ancient practice that has a variety of benefits, including preserving food for long periods of time; however, fermenting does not always improve the taste. Think of really smelly cheese, for example. What are the pros and cons of fermenting food? Do foods in their original state taste better than fermented ones?

Are You Pros or Cons? • Pro ☐   • Con ☐

A Make two groups: pros and cons. Come up with a supporting argument for your position on the given topic. Follow the reasoning method provided below.

What Do the Majority Think?
Define the objective criteria
▸

What Do You Think?
Define the subjective criteria
▸

Narrowing Criteria
What are the pros to these criteria?
▸

What are the cons to these criteria?
▸

Coming Up With an Argument:

Final Opinion
▸

B Discuss your supporting ideas with the opposing group. All members of the group should participate in giving and answering the questions.

Phrase Bank

• **Contributing Ideas**

☐ How about…?
☐ Maybe we could….
☐ What about this…?
☐ To reach our goal, we could try….
☐ To get a range of ideas, why don't we…?
☐ Thinking inside the box could lead us to….
☐ Thinking outside the box could lead us to….
☐ To challenge conventions, let's assume….
☐ Switching gears, let's consider the issue from a new angle.
☐ Let's brainstorm first and judge later.

• **Encouraging Ideas**

☐ Brilliant! / I like that! / Awesome! / Good thinking!

• **Expanding on Ideas**

☐ That gives me an idea.
☐ Another idea would be….
☐ Yeah, we could also….

Active Discussion 1

5. Fun Forum

Q1 Armchair Traveler

Where have you been in the world? Form small groups and discuss where people have been before. Find out the travel experiences of your group. Write the names of the countries your group has visited below.

Visited Countries:
_____
_____
_____
_____

Q2 Culture Shock!

Now interview each other about different cultures the members have visited before. Most importantly, ask about the culture shock members have experienced in other cultures. Ask them specifically the reason for their culture shock.

Fill out the form below:

Names	What Other Culture(s) Have You Visited?	Culture Shock Experience and Reasons

** Culture shock: A state of bewilderment experienced by an individual who is suddenly exposed to a new, strange, or foreign cultural environment.

A Sneak Peek!

If you were a host to a Roundtable Discussion program, what would you ask about the following topic? Write three questions and discuss about it.

[The Effects of Stress and How to Manage It]

1. _____

2. _____

3. _____

Lesson 05 / Fermented Food: Cheese or Fermented Soybeans?

Issue 2: Daily Lives

1 Word Power

The bold words provided are from the articles in this issue. Circle the synonyms and underline the antonyms.

• civilized	Enlightened	Advanced	Inexperienced	Knowledgeable	Accomplished
• combine	Disconnect	Merge	Link	Associate	Separate
• desire	Ambition	Aversion	Longing	Indifference	Rapture
• essential	Secondary	Fundamental	Vital	Indispensible	Auxiliary
• serendipitously	Unintentionally	Spontaneously	Deliberately	Painstakingly	Accidentally
• purported	Alleged	Implied	True	Apparent	Actual

2 Thinking it Over

A Voice Your Opinion

Let's rethink about the discussion questions from the lessons of this issue. Consolidate your discussion skills while giving opinions to the discussion questions below.

1) When do you use perfume, and what do you hope it will do for you or others?

2) How important is wearing perfume to you, and what kind of scents do you like?

3) What kind and how many different memories do perfume scents create for you?

4) What is your favorite kind of cheese? What sort of flavor does it have?

5) How important is eating healthily to you? What types of food do you think should be included in a healthy diet?

B Phrase Banks Review

Rephrase the underlined expressions and then rewrite the sentences.

1) Introducing Your Experience

- <u>Let me tell you about one of my worst experiences</u> trying some really pungent Dutch cheese.

  ....

- <u>One of my best experiences was when</u> I went to a shop where you could mix your own fragrances. It was amazing.

  ....

2) Beginning the Discussion

- <u>Let's talk about</u> our experiences trying different fermented foods.

  ....

- <u>Should we begin with</u> discussing our first experiences purchasing perfume?

  ....

3) Contributing Ideas

- <u>To get a range of ideas, why don't we</u> each share some of our favorite memories about perfume?

  ....

- <u>How about</u> sharing some of the things you look for in a new perfume?

  ....

4) Encouraging Ideas

- <u>Good thinking!</u> I agree with your point about perfumes changing with people's personal scents.

  ....

- <u>Brilliant!</u> I never thought that fermented tofu could taste this great!

  ....

5) Expanding on Ideas

- <u>Another idea would be</u> to share our personal opinions about different fermented foods.

  ....

- <u>Yeah, we could also</u> discuss how we pick fragrances for different occasions.

  ....

Excellent! Now You are Ready to Go Onto the Next Topic! ⟹

LESSON 06

Food Crisis

Learning Objectives
After completing this lesson, you will be able to…

- Give logical opinions about global food crisis and actions to combat worldwide famine.
- Utilize useful discussion phrases regarding interrupting and disagreeing with different positions.

1. Warming Up!

A *Check* the words you know and *circle* the words that you do not yet know.

Voca-space

vulnerable	hunger pangs	premature
recession	potential	consequences
malnutrition	famine	domestic
demand	expanding	urgent
intervention	stunt	tackle
nutrition	substantial	

B In groups, help each other to find the meaning of the circled words. The dictionary should be the last resort!

2. Making a Case [A]

Read the article below. Gather ideas about the topic as you read the article.

The Global Food Crisis

You might **be surprised to learn that** even in the twenty-first century hunger is considered to be the greatest health risk to face mankind—with an **impact even greater than** common diseases like AIDS and malaria combined. Currently, experts estimate that one in eight people across the globe does not get enough to eat.

Beyond simple **hunger pangs**, malnutrition **causes a variety of** serious **health problems** to its sufferers. These include an increased risk of disease and even **premature** death. For young victims, the **consequences** of **malnutrition** can **shape the rest of their lives**. Not getting the necessary **nutrition** can physically and mentally **stunt** children—**something that limits** their **potential** as they continue to grow.

Hunger affects people worldwide, with approximately three-quarters of those suffering living in rural areas in developing countries. **In recent years**, the problem has worsened due to rising food prices and the spread of the global **recession**. Of the estimated 870 million malnourished people worldwide, more than three-quarters live in the Asia and Pacific regions and in Sub-Saharan Africa. This is not just a problem for the heavily affected countries, but for all members of the **global community**.

A Stretch Your Thinking

In groups, brainstorm ideas and opinions about the topic on the provided mind map. The provided keywords from [A] are to be used as starting points.

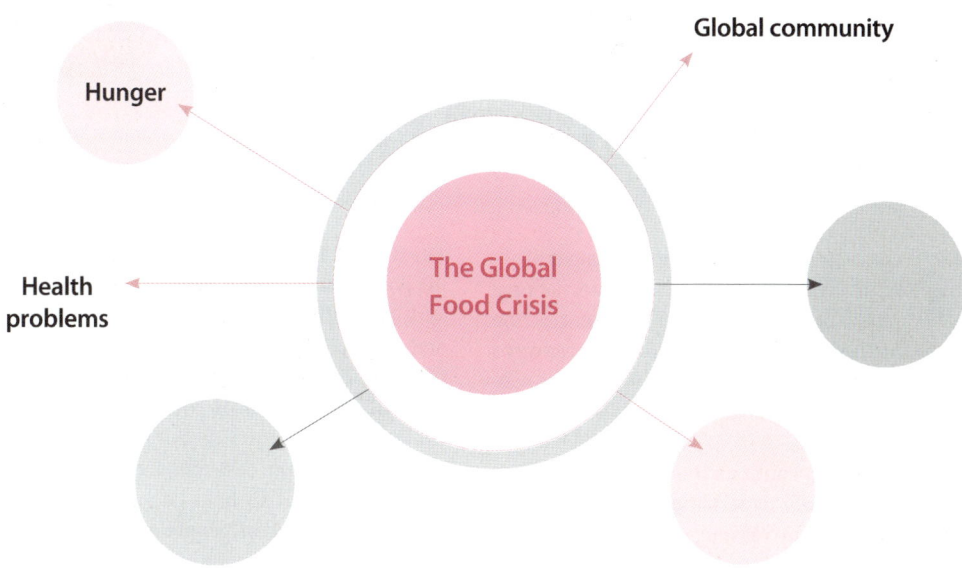

B Phrase Fit

be surprised to learn that	something that limits
impact even greater than	causes a variety of
shape the rest of their lives	in recent years

Fill in the blanks using the above expressions to complete the sentences which are about [A].

1) In addition to feeling hungry, malnutrition _____ health issues to those affected by it.

2) _____, poor economic conditions worldwide have caused the global food crisis to spread.

3) You might _____ even in modern times malnutrition is a bigger threat than illnesses such as AIDS and malaria combined.

C True or False?

Circle TRUE if the statement corresponds with [A]; if not, circle FALSE.

1) Hunger is a problem that has been greatly reduced in recent years.
(TRUE / FALSE)

2) Hunger is thought of as the biggest health problem worldwide and affects more people than some infectious diseases.
(TRUE / FALSE)

Correct and rewrite each false statement below.

_____

_____

_____

_____

Lesson 06 / Food Crisis   53

2. Making a Case [B]

Read the article below. Gather ideas about the topic as you read the article.

A Need for Global Effort to Combat Famine

Given the large scale of the global hunger problem, many world leaders and international organizations are calling for **urgent** action to **tackle** the food crisis. There are **growing concerns that famine** might spread to hit millions of poor people worldwide if a **solution** is not found.

As prices of grain continue to rise due to growing **demand** from rapidly **expanding** economies, many people are finding it increasingly difficult to **put food on the table**.

A solution to the growing food crisis is the World Bank's Global Food Crisis Response Program (GFRP). The GFRP's solution involves closing borders, providing government **intervention** in food and input markets, and **other actions that boost** social protection and the maintenance of **domestic** short-term food production. As a result, **resources have benefited** 65.9 million people in 49 countries.

However, recent research indicates that **without substantial effort** to help people in **vulnerable** regions, the number of people at **risk** for hunger will increase 20 percent by 2050. For this reason, nations worldwide **must band together** to combat this growing global problem.

A Stretch Your Thinking

In groups, brainstorm ideas and opinions about the topic on the provided mind map. The provided keywords from [B] are to be used as starting points.

54 | Active Discussion 1

B Phrase Fit

other actions that boost	put food on the table
without substantial effort	must band together
growing concerns that famine	resources have benefited

Fill in the blanks using the above expressions to complete the sentences which are about [B].

1) To effectively combat global famine, organizations and governments across the globe _____ to find a solution.

2) A solution provided by the World Bank includes the maintenance of domestic food production and _____ _____ social protection.

3) However, there are _____ _____ will only continue to grow if help is not provided.

C True or False?

Circle TRUE if the statement corresponds with [B]; if not, circle FALSE.

1) The World Bank's Global Food Crisis Response Program helped millions of famished people worldwide.
(TRUE / FALSE)

2) Increased demand from growing economies is causing the prices of grain to rise worldwide.
(TRUE / FALSE)

Correct and rewrite each false statement below.

_____
_____
_____
_____

3. What's Your Opinion?

Share your opinions about the discussion questions below using the provided useful expressions from the Phrase Bank as much as possible.

1) Is it possible to fairly distribute food to people who are starving around the world? Why or why not?

2) Do you normally have a lot of food leftover after meals? How can we stop wasting food?

3) How do you feel when you hear news about famines in other countries?

4) Have you ever donated food or money to help in a poor country? Why or why not? Give specific reasons.

5) What do you think is the best way to help people suffering from hunger worldwide?

Phrase Bank

• **Interrupting**
☐ I'm sorry to cut you off, but….
☐ I'm sorry to interrupt, but….
☐ Excuse me for interrupting, but….
☐ Let's not discuss (topic) any further.
☐ Let's break off our discussion.

• **Disagreeing with Positions**
☐ That certainly is one possibility, but….
☐ I'm not so sure about that because….
☐ That might be true, but….
☐ A lot of people might agree with that, but….

4. Raise the Issues!

Pros & Cons

Is Food Aid a Better than Food Production Education?

Hunger is a problem that affects millions of people worldwide. There is no easy long-term solution. Is giving immediate help in the form of food donations a better solution than teaching people skills necessary to help them more efficiently produce food on their own?

Are You Pros or Cons? • Pro ☐   • Con ☐

A Make two groups: pros and cons. Come up with a supporting argument for your position on the given topic. Follow the reasoning method provided below.

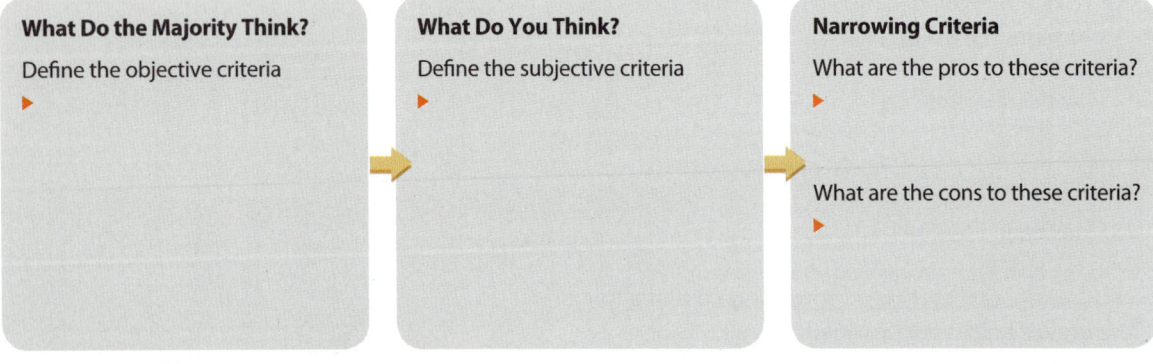

What Do the Majority Think?
Define the objective criteria
▸

What Do You Think?
Define the subjective criteria
▸

Narrowing Criteria
What are the pros to these criteria?
▸

What are the cons to these criteria?
▸

Coming Up With an Argument:

Final Opinion
▸

B Discuss your supporting ideas with the opposing group. All members of the group should participate in giving and answering the questions.

Phrase Bank

• **Interrupting**
☐ I'm sorry to cut you off, but….
☐ I'm sorry to interrupt, but….
☐ Excuse me for interrupting, but….
☐ Let's not discuss (topic) any further.
☐ Let's break off our discussion.

• **Disagreeing with Positions**
☐ That certainly is one possibility, but….
☐ I'm not so sure about that because….
☐ That might be true, but….
☐ A lot of people might agree with that, but….

5. Fun Forum

Fate or Free Will?

Q1 Do you believe in fate? If yes, explain your reasons for believing in fate. If not, explain your reasons for believing in free will.

_____
_____
_____

Q2 Now gather into groups of two or more. Compare your reasons for believing in fate or free will with others. How are they different? How are they similar?

_____
_____
_____

A Sneak Peek!

If you were a host to a Roundtable Discussion program, what would you ask about the following topic? Write three questions and discuss about it.

[Donating Organs]

1. _____

2. _____

3. _____

07 ★ Culture Lab

Beautiful Comradeships

- **Learning Objectives**

After completing this lesson, you will be able to...

- Give logical opinions about organ donations and related cultural factors.
- Utilize useful discussion phrases regarding defending positions and agreeing with others' positions.

1. Warming Up!

A *Check* the words you know and *circle* the words that you do not yet know.

Voca-space

invaluable	whole	reliable
donate	tradition	shortage
participation	respect	decision
comfortable	reluctance	consent
opt-in/opt-out	commit	acceptable
organ transplants		

B In groups, help each other to find the meaning of the circled words. The dictionary should be the last resort!

2. Making a Case [A]

Read the article below. Gather ideas about the topic as you read the article.

Donating Life

For centuries, doctors have experimented with **organ transplants**; however, it is only in the last hundred years that the surgeries have become **reliable** enough **to become common practice**. Thanks to organ transplants, it is possible to save the **lives of many people** with medical conditions that would have been death sentences a hundred years ago.

At the moment, most countries have a **shortage of organs for transplantation**. This has led to government policies that encourage organ donation. **Some countries favor** the "opt-in" system (people must actively choose to **donate**,) while others use the "opt-out" system (**consent** is assumed unless you say no.) This can **cause huge differences in** donor **participation**. For example, compare Germany, where 12% of the population is opt-in donors, with Austria, where 99% of the population is assumed to be willing donors.

Organ donation is an **invaluable** gift that can save many lives. Although many organs must be donated after death, some things like kidneys and partial organs can be taken from living donors. For this rea-son, people worldwide **have the option to choose** both during life and after death to give part of themselves to those in need.

58 | Active Discussion 1

A Stretch Your Thinking

In groups, brainstorm ideas and opinions about the topic on the provided mind map. The provided keywords from [A] are to be used as starting points.

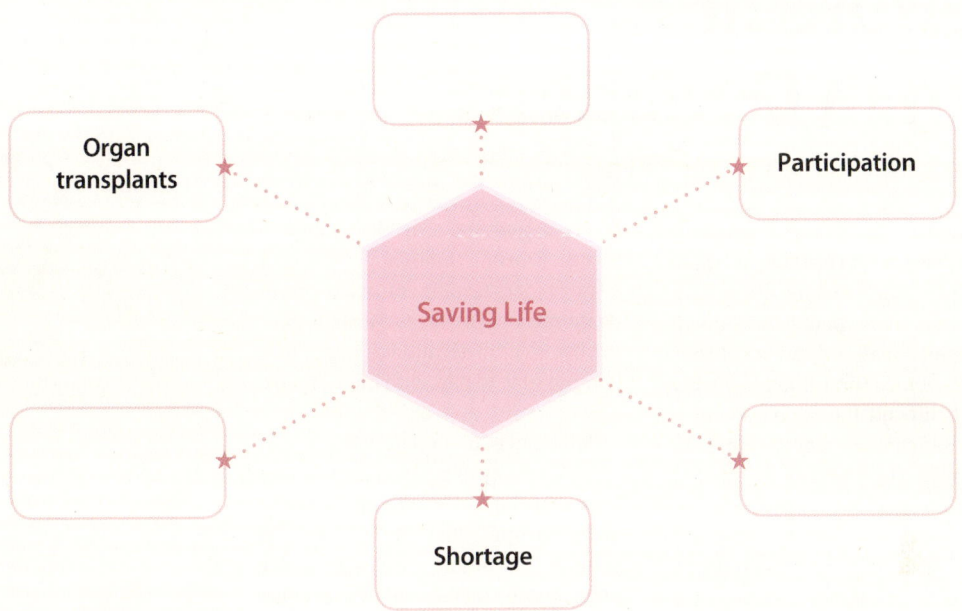

B Phrase Fit

to become common practice	shortage of organs for transplantation
some countries favor	lives of many people
have the option to choose	cause huge differences in

Fill in the blanks using the above expressions to complete the sentences which are about [A].

1) At the moment, people _____ to donate their organs both during their lifetime and after death.

2) The _____ has led to government policies that are aimed at encouraging people to donate organs.

3) In the last century, organ transplant surgeries have become safe and dependable enough _____.

C True or False?

Circle TRUE if the statement corresponds with [A]; if not, circle FALSE.

1) More people participate in opt-in organ donation programs than opt-out.
(TRUE / FALSE)

2) Organ transplants save the lives of people with serious health conditions.
(TRUE / FALSE)

Correct and rewrite each false statement below.

_____
_____
_____
_____

Lesson 07 / Beautiful Comradeships

2. Making a Case [B]

Read the article below. Gather ideas about the topic as you read the article.

Culture of Organ Donations

In modern times, organ donation has become **acceptable** in many cultures and religions around the world. In general, people worldwide view organ donation as **an act of charity**; however, cultural differences **can make it difficult for** people living in some countries to feel **comfortable** giving away their organs or those of their loved ones.

Some Asian nations like China, Japan, and the Philippines share a **tradition** of holding onto organs after death. **The most common reasons for** this tradition are the belief that the removal of an organ violates the sanctity of the deceased, the desire to be buried **whole**, a dislike of organs living on inside another person, and a misunderstanding of what brain death means. For these reasons, people living in these cultures might find it impossible to part with their organs.

Reluctance to donate organs can cause a variety of problems, including organ shortages. **Despite the benefits**, many people find it difficult to **commit** to organ donation. **Over time, these beliefs** might change. But, it is important to remember that the **decision** tto donate organs is a very personal one. Whether you're donating yours or a loved one's, this decision **needs to be treated with respect.**

A Stretch Your Thinking

In groups, brainstorm ideas and opinions about the topic on the provided mind map. The provided keywords from [B] are to be used as starting points.

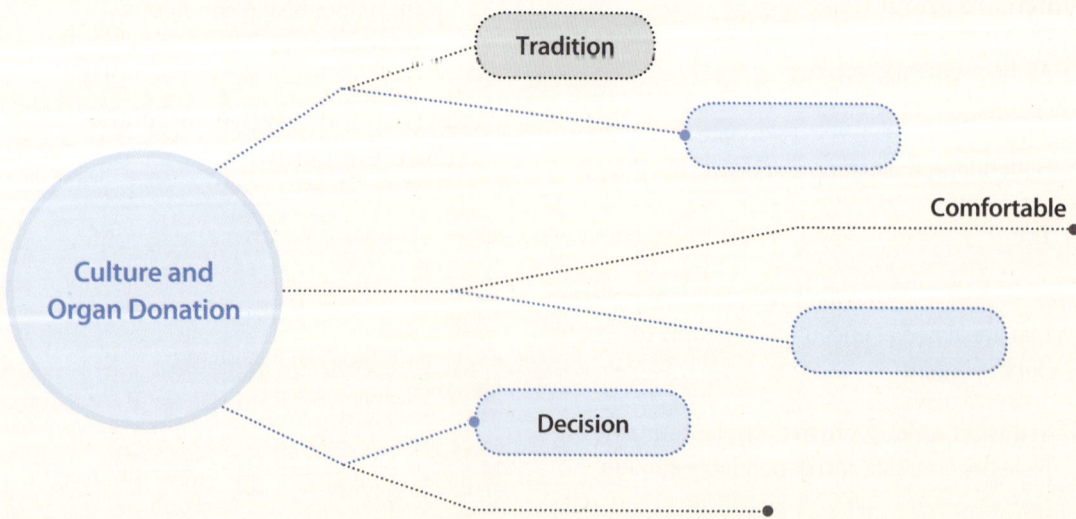

B Phrase Fit

an act of charity	can make it difficult for
despite the benefits	over time these beliefs
the most common reasons for	needs to be treated with respect

Fill in the blanks using the above expressions to complete the sentences which are about [B].

1) _____, many people face difficulties when considering organ donations.

2) Cultural factors _____ some people to donate their organs or those of their loved ones.

3) Some of _____ rejecting organ donation are a desire to keep the human body whole after death and discomfort about organs continuing to live in the bodies of others.

C True or False?

Circle TRUE if the statement corresponds with [B]; if not, circle FALSE.

1) Some people are uncomfortable with organ donation due to cultural and religious factors. (TRUE / FALSE)

2) The article argues that people in many countries refuse to donate organs because it can spread disease. (TRUE / FALSE)

Correct and rewrite each false statement below.

_____
_____
_____
_____

3. What's Your Opinion?

Share your opinions about the discussion questions below using the provided useful expressions from the Phrase Bank as much as possible.

1) Would you donate your organs to be used by another person after you die? Give specific reasons to support your answer.

2) Why do some people think of organ donation as the gift of life?

3) How can we encourage more people to donate organs? Be specific.

4) Do you know anyone who has given or received an organ?

5) Is organ donation widespread in your country? Why or why not? Give specific reasons.

Phrase Bank

• Defending Positions
☐ Let me put it another way….
☐ I think the point I'm trying to make here is….
☐ Well, if you could just spare me a moment,….
☐ Understanding the idea requires deliberation.
☐ To elucidate the idea,….
☐ The crux of the issue is….

• Agreeing with Positions
☐ I'd have to agree that….
☐ I think that's a good point.
☐ Sure/Right/Certainly/Absolutely/Exactly
☐ That's all right.
☐ What you're saying may be right.
☐ It sounds good.

4. Raise the Issues!

Pros & Cons

To Donate or Not to Donate

Organ donation is a very private decision. The choice involves many factors like personal preference and cultural background. There are many reasons to be for or against organ donation (e.g. for- giving others a chance at life; against- losing a part of yourself). Are the reasons to be for organ donation more convincing than reasons to be against it?

Are You Pros or Cons? • Pro ☐ • Con ☐

A Make two groups: pros and cons. Come up with a supporting argument for your position on the given topic. Follow the reasoning method provided below.

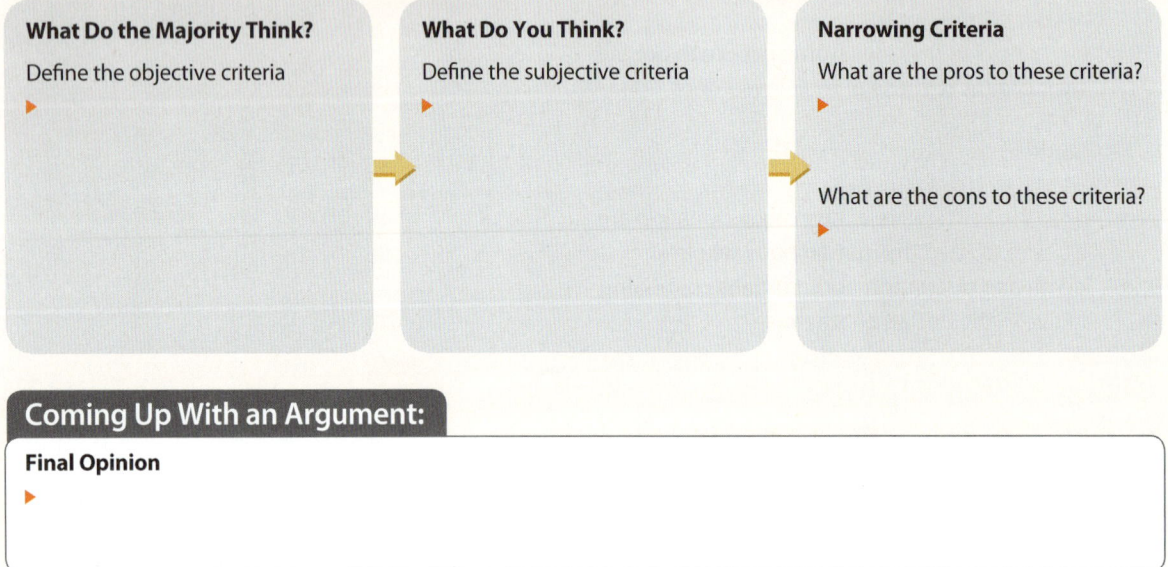

What Do the Majority Think?	What Do You Think?	Narrowing Criteria
Define the objective criteria	Define the subjective criteria	What are the pros to these criteria?
		What are the cons to these criteria?

Coming Up With an Argument:

Final Opinion
▶

B Discuss your supporting ideas with the opposing group. All members of the group should participate in giving and answering the questions.

Phrase Bank

• Defending Positions
- ☐ Let me put it another way….
- ☐ I think the point I'm trying to make here is….
- ☐ Well, if you could just spare me a moment,….
- ☐ Understanding the idea requires deliberation.
- ☐ To elucidate the idea,….
- ☐ The crux of the issue is….

• Agreeing with Positions
- ☐ I'd have to agree that….
- ☐ I think that's a good point.
- ☐ Sure/Right/Certainly/Absolutely/Exactly
- ☐ That's all right.
- ☐ What you're saying may be right.
- ☐ It sounds good.

5. Fun Forum

① If you could choose to devote your life to a single cause, what would it be? Why did you pick that cause? Give specific reasons.

② Now discuss your chosen cause with your group members. Interview other members about what they would like to devote their life to. Are their choices similar to yours? How are they different?

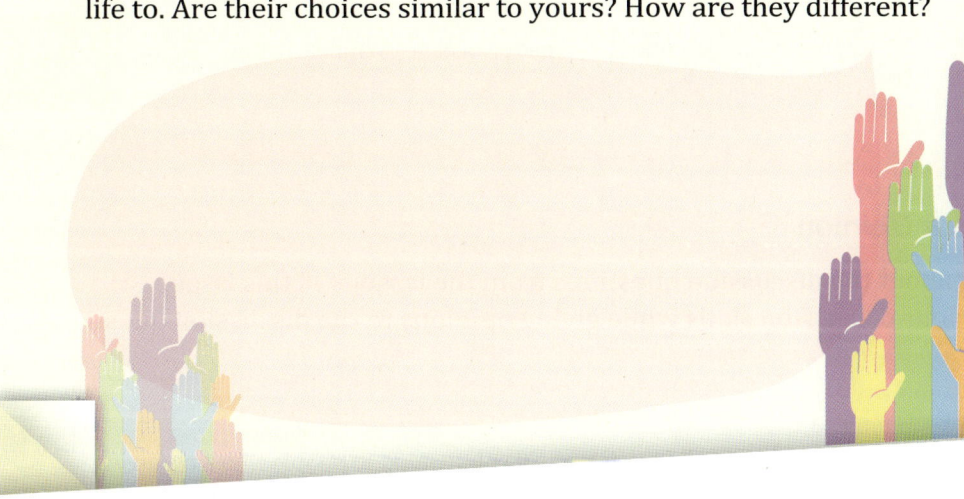

A Sneak Peek!

If you were a host to a Roundtable Discussion program, what would you ask about the following topic? Write three questions and discuss about it.

[Expiration Date on Romantic Love?]

1.

2.

3.

Issue 3: Ethics

1 Word Power

The bold words provided are from the articles in this issue. Circle the synonyms and underline the antonyms.

• substantial	Insignificant	Momentous	Considerable	Miniscule	Generous
• urgent	Pressing	Driving	Compelling	Irrelevant	Critical
• tackle	Ambition	Neglect	Venture	Ignore	Strive
• invaluable	Unconstructive	Instrumental	Significant	Disadvantageous	Adverse
• reluctance	Hesitancy	Qualm	Hostility	Repulsion	Enthusiasm
• reliable	Deceptive	Conscientious	Unequivocal	Unimpeachable	Rash

2 Thinking it Over

A Voice Your Opinion

Let's rethink about the discussion questions from the lessons of this issue. Consolidate your discussion skills while giving opinions to the discussion questions below.

1) Is it possible to fairly distribute food to people who are starving around the world? Why or why not?

2) What do you think is the best way to help people suffering from hunger worldwide?

3) Would you donate your organs to be used by another person after you die? Give specific reasons to support your answer.

4) Why do some people think of organ donation as the gift of life?

5) Is organ donation widespread in your country? Why or why not? Give specific reasons.

B Phrase Banks Review

Rephrase the underlined expressions and then rewrite the sentences.

1) Interrupting

- **I'm sorry to cut you off, but** I don't think the hunger problem will be that easily solved.

....

2) Disagreeing with Positions

- **That certainly is one possibility, but** try to see the issue from the side of people who need organs.

....

- **I'm not sure about that because** there is no evidence to support that claim.

....

3) Defending Positions

- **Let me put it another way**: I think all people should be required to donate their organs after death.

....

- **The crux of the issue is** that I think if countries worldwide work together, we will be able to find a way to tackle the hunger crisis.

....

4) Agreeing with Positions

- **I'd have to agree that** our society should consider the hunger problems of other nations before wasting food.

....

- **What you're saying may be right.** Organ donation is like giving a gift to someone in need.

....

- **That's all right.** I agree that a collective effort is necessary to help those suffering from hunger.

....

Excellent! Now You are Ready to Go Onto the Next Topic!

08 LESSON

Expiration Date on Love?

- **Learning Objectives**

After completing this lesson, you will be able to…

- Give logical opinions about love and how to sustain a soul-mate relationship.
- Utilize useful discussion phrases regarding suggesting options, rejecting options, and asking others to reconsider.

1. Warming Up!

A *Check* the words you know and *circle* the words that you do not yet know.

Voca-space

social chemistry	romantic	fade	secure
tremendous	woo	marital	elude
extinguish	therapist	vigor	passion
sustaining	foundation		

B In groups, help each other to find the meaning of the circled words. The dictionary should be the last resort!

2. Making a Case [A]

Read the article below. Gather ideas about the topic as you read the article.

The Science of Love

Italian scientists have discovered a chemical in the brain that causes **romantic** feelings. This chemical is believed to **fade over the course of** a year. This might explain why the giddy, **head-over-heels in love** feeling that we have at the start of a new relationship decreases over time.

Researchers from the University of Pavia found that levels of a protein called **Nerve Growth Factor** (NGF) greatly increase when a person first falls in love. High NGF levels come from a rush of adrenalin. This causes people **to feel renewed vigor**, confidence, and a **lust for life** as their new love grows. Levels of NGF greatly decrease over a year or so as people become more **secure** in their new relationship.

They found that NGF has an important role in the **social chemistry** of human beings. When NGF levels are high, there is also **an urgency to** constantly **woo** a potential partner to ensure that they are yours. Although NGF decreases over time, the bonding that **occurs in this stage** creates a good **foundation** for the relationship to continue on.

A Stretch Your Thinking

In groups, brainstorm ideas and opinions about the topic on the provided mind map. The provided keywords from **[A]** are to be used as starting points.

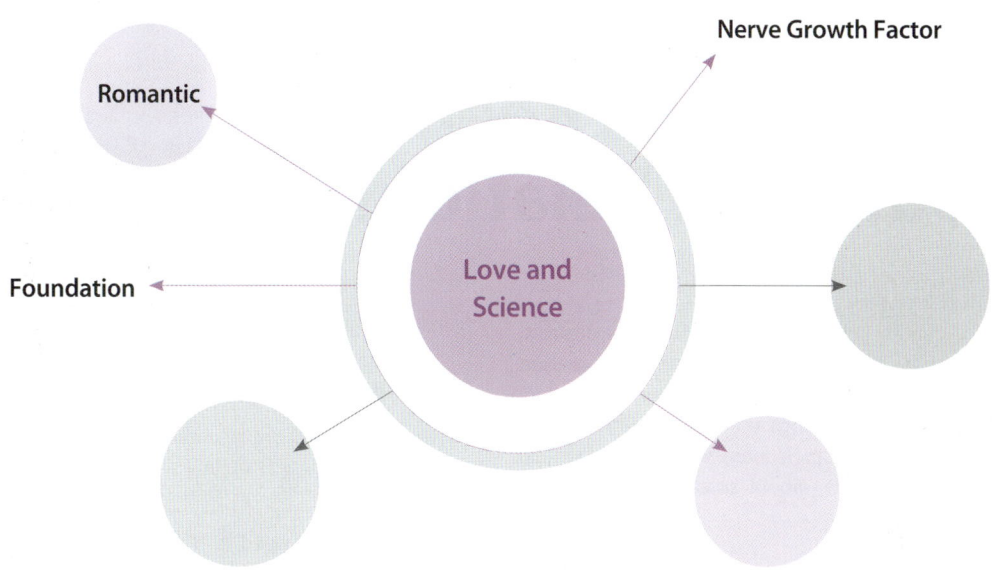

B Phrase Fit

over the course of	an urgency to
occurs in this stage	head-over-heels in love
to feel renewed vigor	lust for life

Fill in the blanks using the above expressions to complete the sentences which are about **[A]**.

1) At the start of a new relationship, people feel .... seduce their potential partner to make sure that they share the same feelings.

2) Most people fall .... at the start of a new relationship.

3) Levels of NGF are thought to decrease .... a one-year period.

C True or False?

Circle TRUE if the statement corresponds with **[A]**; if not, circle FALSE.

1) As Nerve Growth Factor (NGF) decreases, feelings of love disappear.
   (TRUE / FALSE)

2) High NGF levels are caused by eating too much protein.   (TRUE / FALSE)

Correct and rewrite each false statement below.

....

....

....

....

Lesson 08 / Expiration Date on Love?

2. Making a Case [B]

Read the article below. Gather ideas about the topic as you read the article.

Forever and Always: How-To's on Keeping a Soul-mate Relationship

Human beings have a **tremendous** desire to love and be loved. Yet, **meaningful relationships with** the opposite sex often **elude** us. Here are some **things that I have learned** in my life—as a divorced single mom, widow, and a woman remarried after 50—about **sustaining** a soul-mate relationship:

1. Know who you are and what you want. You have to know yourself to know what you want in a partner.
2. Learn to disagree. Avoiding conflict **extinguishes passion** and **can lead to** the death of a marriage.
3. Do not value your children over your **marital** relationship. Someday, it will just be the two of you again. **Be sure you** still know each other.
4. Remember the other person cannot read your mind. Be a big girl or boy and ask for what you want!
5. Get help **if you need it**. If your relationship is in trouble, **seek out ways to** make it better. Find a relationship coach, a **therapist**, a marriage counselor, or a book.
6. Most importantly, if you have a soul-mate, never take your relationship for granted.

A Stretch Your Thinking

In groups, brainstorm ideas and opinions about the topic on the provided mind map. The provided keywords from [B] are to be used as starting points.

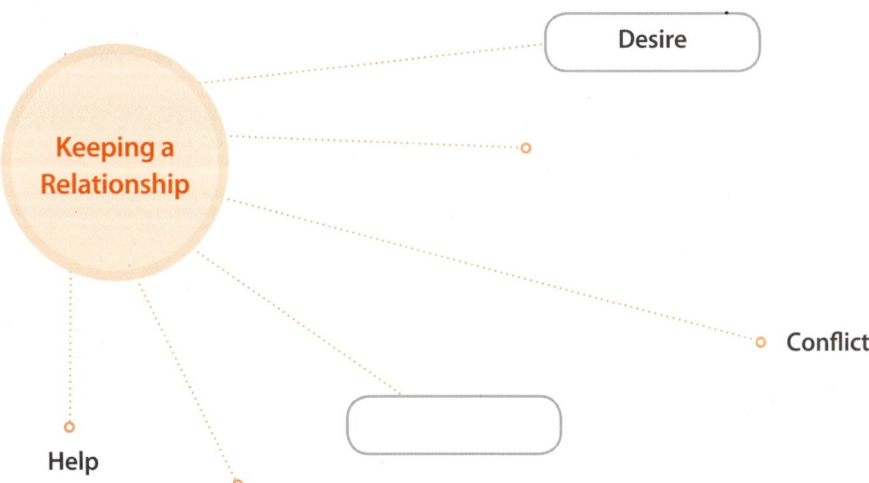

B Phrase Fit

meaningful relationships with	if you need it
things that I have learned	can lead to
be sure you	seek out ways to

Fill in the blanks using the above expressions to complete the sentences which are about **[B]**.

1) If you are having marital problems, don't be afraid to ask others for help _____ _____.

2) Bottling up anger causes passion to disappear from your relationship and _____ marriage failure.

3) I want to share some _____ _____ about finding and keeping a soul-mate in my 50 years of life experience.

C True or False?

Circle TRUE if the statement corresponds with **[B]**; if not, circle FALSE.

1) The writer of this article thinks children are the most important part of a marriage.
(TRUE / FALSE)

2) In the article, the author says it is important to ask for what you want from your husband or wife. (TRUE / FALSE)

Correct and rewrite each false statement below.

_____
_____
_____
_____
_____

3. What's Your Opinion?

Share your opinions about the discussion questions below using the provided useful expressions from the Phrase Bank as much as possible.

1) Do you feel confident asking for what you want in a relationship? Is it okay to do this in your culture?

2) Do you think it is true that romantic love lasts only one year? Give specific reasons to support your answer.

3) What things do you think are most important in a relationship? Be specific.

4) Which of the author's tips in Case B do you like best? Can you think of any more tips on sustaining a relationship?

5) What is your definition of love? Be specific.

Phrase Bank

- **Suggesting Options**
  - ☐ Would this be okay?
  - ☐ Would this work?
  - ☐ Would this fit our criteria?
  - ☐ What if we did this?

- **Rejecting Options**
  - ☐ I don't think that would work because….
  - ☐ We don't see eye to eye on….
  - ☐ I don't share your view on….

- **Asking to Reconsider**
  - ☐ Why don't you think it over?
  - ☐ Please reconsider.
  - ☐ Could you think further about that?
  - ☐ Don't jump to conclusions.

4. Raise the Issues!

Pros & Cons

Is Finding New Love Better than Sustaining a Soul-mate Relationship?

Relationships go through many stages. At the beginning, everything is exciting and new. After a few years, things become comfortable and secure. Is the passionate beginning stage of the relationship better than the relaxed soul-mate stage?

Are You Pros or Cons? • Pro ☐   • Con ☐

A Make two groups: pros and cons. Come up with a supporting argument for your position on the given topic. Follow the reasoning method provided below.

What Do the Majority Think?	What Do You Think?	Narrowing Criteria
Define the objective criteria ▸	Define the subjective criteria ▸	What are the pros to these criteria? ▸
		What are the cons to these criteria? ▸

Coming Up With an Argument:

Final Opinion
▸

B Discuss your supporting ideas with the opposing group. All members of the group should participate in giving and answering the questions.

Phrase Bank

• Suggesting Options	• Rejecting Options	• Asking to Reconsider
☐ Would this be okay?	☐ I don't think that would work because….	☐ Why don't you think it over?
☐ Would this work?	☐ We don't see eye to eye on….	☐ Please reconsider.
☐ Would this fit our criteria?	☐ I don't share your view on….	☐ Could you think further about that?
☐ What if we did this?		☐ Don't jump to conclusions.

Active Discussion 1

5. Fun Forum

Apple of My Eye

Q1 What factors are important in choosing a partner? Be specific and give reasons for your choices.

Q2 Now discuss your ideal factors with other members of your group. How are they different? How are they the same? Write your factors and others' factors in the Venn diagram below. Write the common factors in the middle of the diagram.

My Factors — Others' Factors

A Sneak Peek!

If you were a host to a Roundtable Discussion program, what would you ask about the following topic? Write three questions and discuss about it.

[SNS Relationships]

1.
2.
3.

LESSON 09

Cyber Relationships

- **Learning Objectives**

  After completing this lesson, you will be able to…

- Give logical opinions about online relationships.
- Utilize useful discussion phrases regarding looking for assumptions in opinions, recognizing errors in opinions, and accepting others' options.

1. Warming Up!

A *Check* the words you know and *circle* the words that you do not yet know.

Voca-space

neglect	online platform	interact
isolated	social networks	withering
posts	like-minded	nurturing
widening	voyeuristic	swiftly
popularity	connections	networking
alienated		

B In groups, help each other to find the meaning of the circled words. The dictionary should be the last resort!

2. Making a Case [A]

Read the article below. Gather ideas about the topic as you read the article.

Online Connections

A social networking service (SNS) is an **online platform** that helps users build **social networks** with people who share interests or real-life connections. They provide an easy way to **interact** over the Internet by sharing information such as pictures, **posts**, events, and interests with others in the same network.

SNS have quickly gained in **popularity** worldwide. **Since its creation** in 2004, Facebook has gone on to claim more than a billion members worldwide. New sites have **sprung up like weeds**. Many countries, schools, and even careers have their own unique platforms for connecting **like-minded** people.

There are many reasons to join an SNS. These sites are useful for both **maintaining relationships with** friends and family living far away and for making new **connec-tions** with people from around the world. SNS can help your career by **providing networking opportunities**. They also pro-vide people living in **isolated** areas with **a bigger social pool**—giving them **a better chance of** finding someone to connect with. Whatever your reasons for joining, it is easy to benefit from SNS's connections.

A Stretch Your Thinking

In groups, brainstorm ideas and opinions about the topic on the provided mind map. The provided keywords from [A] are to be used as starting points.

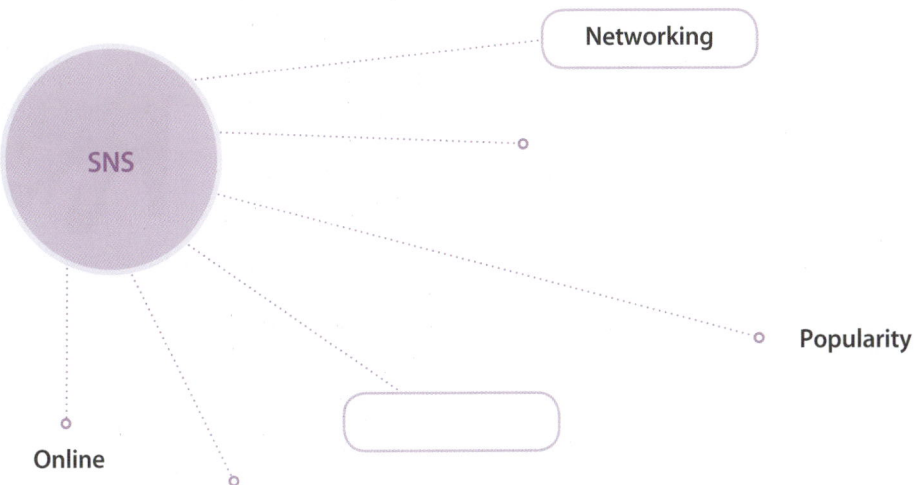

B Phrase Fit

sprung up like weeds	since its creation
providing networking opportunities	giving them a better chance of
a bigger social pool	maintaining relationships with

Fill in the blanks using the above expressions to complete the sentences which are about [A].

1) _____
   Facebook has spread rapidly and can now claim to have more than a billion users around the world.

2) Social networking systems give people living in rural areas a chance to interact with many people worldwide—_____ meeting like-minded people.

3) These services are good for _____ _____ acquaintances living all across the globe.

C True or False?

Circle TRUE if the statement corresponds with [A]; if not, circle FALSE.

1) Social networking sites can help you interact with people in your country only.
   (TRUE / FALSE)

2) You can use social networking services to share pictures, posts, and events with others.
   (TRUE / FALSE)

Correct and rewrite each false statement below.

_____
_____
_____
_____
_____
_____
_____
_____

2. Making a Case [B]

Read the article below. Gather ideas about the topic as you read the article.

Missing Out on Real Relationships

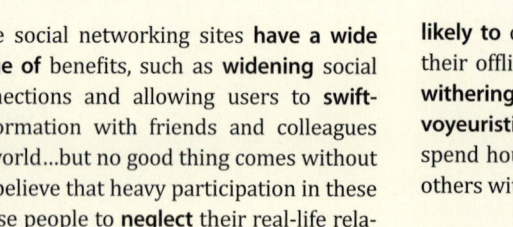

Online social networking sites **have a wide range of** benefits, such as **widening** social connections and allowing users to **swiftly** share information with friends and colleagues around the world…but no good thing comes without a **risk**. Many believe that heavy participation in these sites can cause people to **neglect** their real-life relationships and responsibilities.

Despite SNS sites' claims of connecting users, many people argue that these sites make them feel **alienated from real-life** relationships. Some people have mentioned that using the sites **makes them less likely to** call friends to catch up and that they feel their offline connections to their online friends are **withering** as a result. In addition, some dislike the **voyeuristic** side of these sites where it is possible to spend hours looking at the photos and messages of others without leaving a comment.

Although **it may seem like you are** maintaining relationships, online services **make it all too easy to** hide behind a computer screen and let real-life connections pass you by. For this reason, it is important to **keep a healthy balance between nurturing** your real-life relationships and your online ones.

Ⓐ Stretch Your Thinking

In groups, brainstorm ideas and opinions about the topic on the provided mind map. The provided keywords from [B] are to be used as starting points.

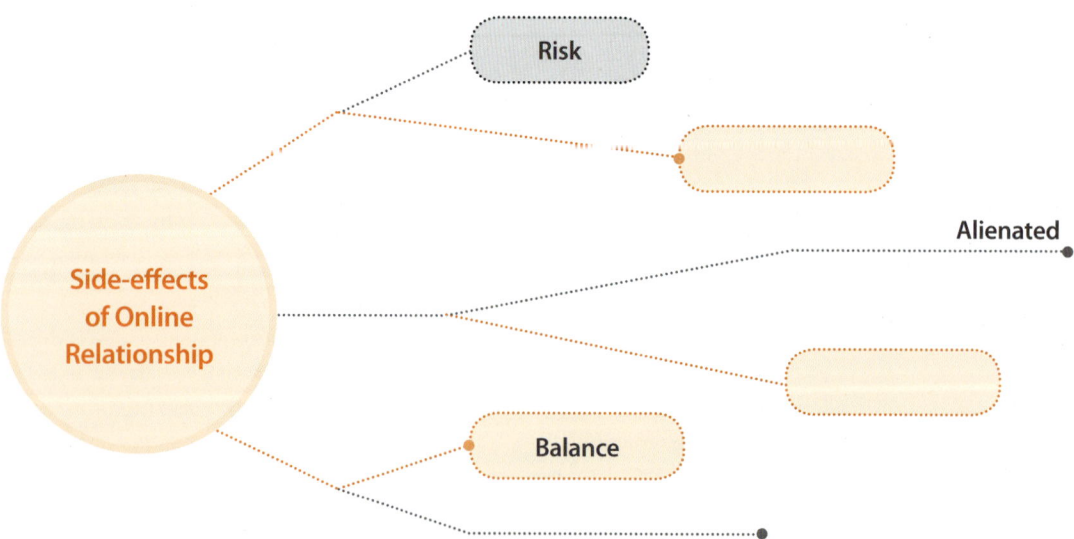

B Phrase Fit

> have a wide range of
> makes them less likely to
> keep a healthy balance between
> alienated from real-life
> it may seem like you are
> make it all too easy to

Fill in the blanks using the above expressions to complete the sentences which are about **[B]**.

1) Although _____ _____ interacting with others, social networking sites may not be a good substitute for real-life interactions.

2) Social networking services _____ _____ benefits, like letting users easily share information with people around the world.

3) In order to maintain mental health, you must try to _____ _____ online interactions and offline ones.

C True or False?

Circle TRUE if the statement corresponds with **[B]**; if not, circle FALSE.

1) SNS can make people feel alienated from their offline relationships.
(TRUE / FALSE)

2) Websites like Facebook are an efficient way to share information and can be a great substitute for talking to people in real life.
(TRUE / FALSE)

Correct and rewrite each false statement below.

_____
_____
_____
_____
_____

3. What's Your Opinion?

Share your opinions about the discussion questions below using the provided useful expressions from the Phrase Bank as much as possible.

1) Do you use any SNS sites regularly? How much time do you spend on SNS every day?

2) What is your favorite SNS site? How did you choose the ones you use?

3) Do you think SNS make you feel closer to your real friends? Give specific reasons.

4) What do you think about people "stalking" other people's profiles (looking at photos and other information without commenting)?

5) Can you remember life before SNS? How has the way you communicate with people changed since then?

Phrase Bank

- **Looking for Assumptions**
  - ☐ We are assuming that….
  - ☐ Is it really necessary that…?
  - ☐ Do we really have to…?
  - ☐ What would happen if we…?

- **Recognizing Errors**
  - ☐ I apologize for my mistake.
  - ☐ It's my fault.

- **Accepting Options**
  - ☐ That would work!
  - ☐ That might be good!
  - ☐ That's a possibility!
  - ☐ That sounds quite convincing to me.
  - ☐ It sounds right to….

4. Raise the Issues!

Pros & Cons

Are SNS Killing Real-World Relationships and Not Improving Them?

There are a lot of benefits to using SNS—connecting friends around the world and helping people connect with like-minded people. However, relying on these services too much can lead to feelings of isolation. Do SNS really just drive people farther apart instead of helping them connect with one another?

Are You Pros or Cons? • Pro ☐ • Con ☐

A Make two groups: pros and cons. Come up with a supporting argument for your position on the given topic. Follow the reasoning method provided below.

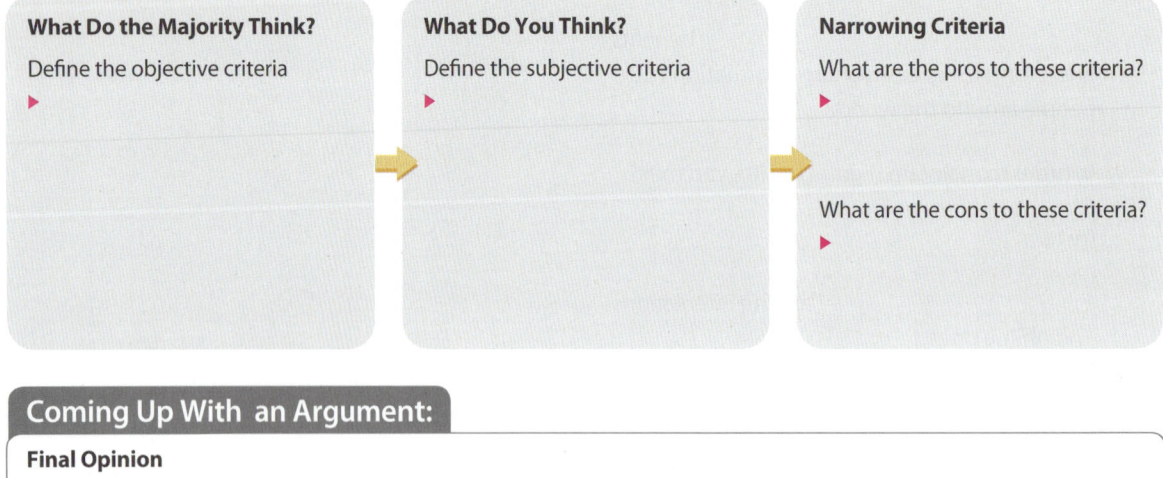

What Do the Majority Think?
Define the objective criteria
▶

What Do You Think?
Define the subjective criteria
▶

Narrowing Criteria
What are the pros to these criteria?
▶

What are the cons to these criteria?
▶

Coming Up With an Argument:

Final Opinion
▶

B Discuss your supporting ideas with the opposing group. All members of the group should participate in giving and answering the questions.

Phrase Bank

• Looking for Assumptions	• Recognizing Errors	• Accepting Options
☐ We are assuming that….	☐ I apologize for my mistake.	☐ That would work!
☐ Is it really necessary that…?	☐ It's my fault.	☐ That might be good!
☐ Do we really have to…?		☐ That's a possibility!
☐ What would happen if we…?		☐ That sounds quite convincing to me.
		☐ It sounds right to….

5. Fun Forum

Captivating People

Q1 Who was the most interesting person you have ever met?

_____
_____
_____
_____
_____

Q2 Now, on the left, make a list of the interesting people that your group members have met. Then, on the right, rewrite the names of the people from the list on the left in the order of who you would most like to meet. Give reasons for your choices.

Most Captivating People	People I Would Like To Meet
1.	1.
2.	2.
3.	3.

A Sneak Peek!

If you were a host to a Roundtable Discussion program, what would you ask about the following topic? Write three questions and discuss about it.

[Eating Alone, Something to be Embarrassed About?]

1.
2.
3.

Lesson 09 / Cyber Relationships

10 ★ Culture Lab

Collectivism and Individualism in Dining

- **Learning Objectives**
  After completing this lesson, you will be able to…

- Give logical opinions about cultural differences in dining in terms of group dining versus one-person dining.
- Utilize useful discussion phrases regarding restating the options, expressing similar instances, and pointing out mistakes.

1. Warming Up!

A *Check* the words you know and *circle* the words that you do not yet know.

Voca-space

lone	communal	embarrassing	serving
prepare	advantage	intimidating	stigma
portions	desperate	individualistic	dining
maximize	collectivist societies		

B In groups, help each other to find the meaning of the circled words. The dictionary should be the last resort!

2. Making a Case [A]

Read the article below. Gather ideas about the topic as you read the article.

Eating Alone is Embarrassing?

In Western **individualistic** countries, it is socially acceptable to eat alone, even at nice restaurants. However, in many places around the world, this type of behavior might be seen as a little odd. For people living in **collectivist societies**, sharing food is a **communal** activity and in many situations, eating alone **might not just be embarrassing**, but also difficult.

In some East Asian countries, like Korea and China, eating is thought of as a social experience and is often used as **a chance for bonding**. As a result, many restaurants might not cater to the individual diner. At many sit-down restaurants, food is sold in **portions** meant to be **shared by a group**. There are also minimum **serving** requirements for some dishes **making it extremely difficult to** eat alone.

Although it is becoming more acceptable to eat alone in many societies around the world, there is still the **risk of feeling uncomfortable** or embarrassed when asking for a table for one. It is important to know which kinds of restaurants accept single diners and **prepare** yourself for **a few sideways glances** by people who might not be as comfortable with the idea as you.

A Stretch Your Thinking

In groups, brainstorm ideas and opinions about the topic on the provided mind map. The provided keywords from [A] are to be used as starting points.

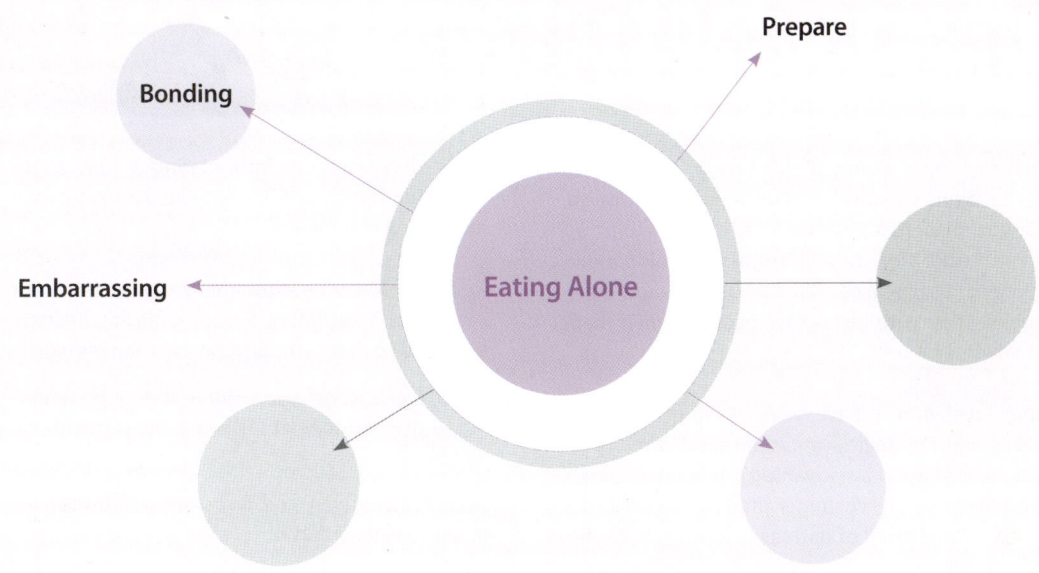

B Phrase Fit

a chance for bonding	a few sideways glances
shared by a group	might not just be
risk of feeling uncomfortable	making it extremely difficult to

Fill in the blanks using the above expressions to complete the sentences which are about [A].

1) When eating alone, be aware of which restaurants accept single customers and be ready for .... from other customers.

2) In some countries in Asia, meals are considered a social time and are often used as ....

3) In some countries, it is normal to share food, and in many restaurants, dining alone .... embarrassing, but it might also be hard.

C True or False?

Circle TRUE if the statement corresponds with [A]; if not, circle FALSE.

1) Eating alone is acceptable and easy to do in every country.
(TRUE / FALSE)

2) In some countries, meals are seen as a social experience and a way to bond with others.
(TRUE / FALSE)

Correct and rewrite each false statement below.

....

....

....

....

Lesson 10 / Collectivism and Individualism in Dining

2. Making a Case [B]

Read the article below. Gather ideas about the topic as you read the article.

Tips for Solo Diners

In today's busy society, it's likely that you will have to eat **alone** sometimes. Plans might **fall through**, or you might just be too tired to bother calling up a friend. **Luckily for you**, the **stigma** of **dining** alone has largely disappeared. Many people are now comfortable eating with just a newspaper to keep them company.

Some restaurants have been cashing in on the **trend** by offering single seats at the bar. At times, eating alone is actually an **advantage**. It is much **easier to find space** for one customer than a party of six. As a result, **a large array of** options is now available for single diners.

Eating alone might be **intimidating** at first, so we have provided some **tips** below to help **maximize** your solo dining experience.

- <u>Research.</u> Not all restaurants have bar areas or seating for **lone** diners. Sitting alone at a huge table could be **more embarrassment than** it's worth.
- <u>Never look embarrassed.</u> While it may be tempting to pretend to wait for someone, you will fool no one.
- <u>Bring something to read.</u> Just **staring off into space** might look **desperate**.

A Stretch Your Thinking

In groups, brainstorm ideas and opinions about the topic on the provided mind map. The provided keywords from [B] are to be used as starting points.

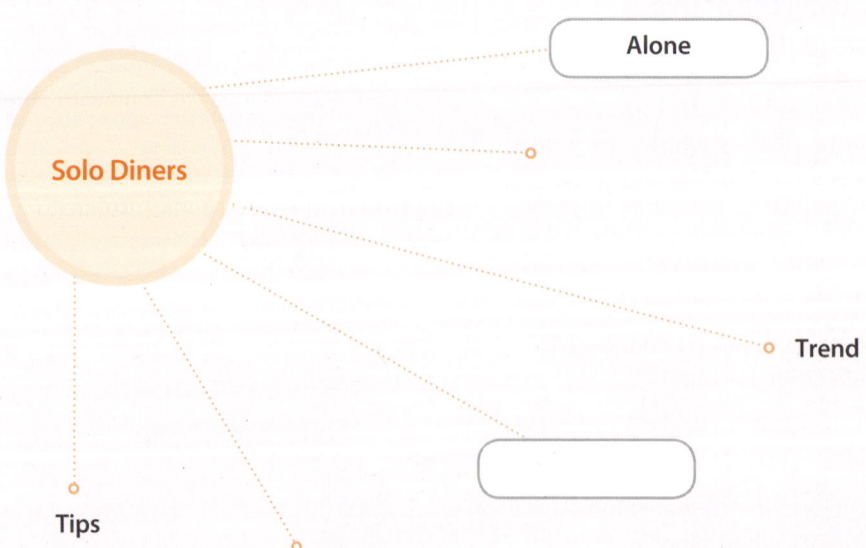

B Phrase Fit

luckily for you	fall through
easier to find space	staring off into space
a large array of	more embarrassment than

Fill in the blanks using the above expressions to complete the sentences which are about **[B]**.

1) Usually, restaurants find it .... for a single diner than a large party.

2) You should always check if restaurants have seating options for single diners because finding yourself alone at a massive table might be .... it's worth.

3) Be sure to bring something to read or do because .... for your entire dinner might make you feel awkward.

C True or False?

Circle TRUE if the statement corresponds with **[B]**; if not, circle FALSE.

1) Recently, many restaurants have been cashing in on the trend of group dining by offering single seats.
(TRUE / FALSE)

2) It's a good idea to bring a book or newspaper to read when you are eating alone.
(TRUE / FALSE)

Correct and rewrite each false statement below.

....
....
....
....

3. What's Your Opinion?

Share your opinions about the discussion questions below using the provided useful expressions from the Phrase Bank as much as possible.

1) Do you often eat alone? Why or why not? Give specific reasons.

2) List three benefits of group dining. Give specific reasons to support your answer.

3) In your country, is it normal to eat alone or eat in groups? Why? Do many restaurants in your country offer one-person seating options?

4) What are some ways to entertain yourself when eating alone? Be specific.

5) What kind of menu would you recommend to a solo diner and to group diners? Be specific.

Phrase Bank

• **Restating the Options**
- ☐ This one has….
- ☐ The advantage of this option is….
- ☐ The disadvantage of this one is….
- ☐ To highlight/emphasize what has been said so far,….
- ☐ To expand upon the points made so far,….

• **Offering a Similar Instance or Expression**
- ☐ In other words,….
- ☐ That is (to say)….
- ☐ …, so to speak,….

• **Pointing Out Mistakes**
- ☐ I'm afraid it was off topic.
- ☐ I don't think you have it quite right.
- ☐ It's unreasonable to say….

4. Raise the Issues!

Pros & Cons

Is Eating Alone Better Than Eating As a Group?

There are good and bad things about eating alone. One disadvatage is having no one to talk with. But, when you're on your own, you can choose when, where, and what to eat without worrying about other people's opinions. It's really a matter of personal preference. Given all these benefits, is eating alone better than eating with others?

Are You Pros or Cons?   • Pro ☐   • Con ☐

A Make two groups: pros and cons. Come up with a supporting argument for your position on the given topic. Follow the reasoning method provided below.

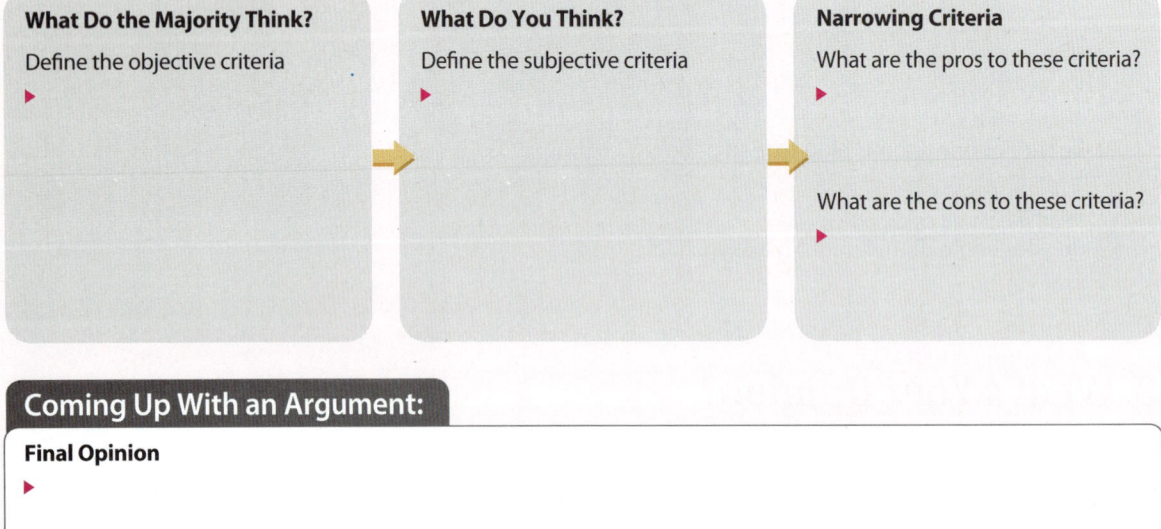

What Do the Majority Think?	**What Do You Think?**	**Narrowing Criteria**
Define the objective criteria ▶	Define the subjective criteria ▶	What are the pros to these criteria? ▶
		What are the cons to these criteria? ▶

Coming Up With an Argument:

Final Opinion
▶

B Discuss your supporting ideas with the opposing group. All members of the group should participate in giving and answering the questions.

Phrase Bank

• Restating the Options	• Offering a Similar Instance or Expression	• Pointing Out Mistakes
☐ This one has….	☐ In other words,….	☐ I'm afraid it was off topic.
☐ The advantage of this option is….	☐ That is (to say)….	☐ I don't think you have it quite right.
☐ The disadvantage of this one is….	☐ …, so to speak,….	☐ It's unreasonable to say….
☐ To highlight/emphasize what has been said so far,….		
☐ To expand upon the points made so far,….		

Active Discussion 1

5. Fun Forum

Stranger than Food

Q1 What is the strangest food you have ever eaten? Be specific about the taste of the food and the ingredients. Why was it so strange?

_____
_____
_____
_____

Q2 Now discuss with your group members about the strangest food they have ever had. Is there any strange food that you would like to try? Give specific reasons to support your answer.

_____
_____
_____
_____

A Sneak Peek!

If you were a host to a Roundtable Discussion program, what would you ask about the following topic? Write three questions and discuss about it.

[Global Warming and Endangered Humans?]

1.

2.

3.

Lesson 10 / Collectivism and Individualism in Dining

Issue 4: Social Lives

1 Word Power

The bold words provided are from the articles in this issue. Circle the synonyms and underline the antonyms.

• **vigor**	Idleness	Endurance	Lethargy	Vehemence	Vitality
• **elude**	Entice	Avoid	Attract	Outwit	Shirk
• **voyeuristic**	Curious	Disinterested	Inquisitive	Indifferent	Peeping
• **isolated**	Deserted	Sequestered	Incorporated	Withdrawn	Stranded
• **stigma**	Credit	Disgrace	Pride	Blemish	Honor
• **communal**	Collective	United	Detached	Single	Individualistic

2 Thinking it Over

A Voice Your Opinion

Let's rethink about the discussion questions from the lessons of this issue. Consolidate your discussion skills while giving opinions to the discussion questions below.

1) Do you often eat alone? Why or why not? Give specific reasons.

2) What are some ways to entertain yourself when eating alone? Be specific.

3) Do you think SNS make you feel closer to your real friends? Give specific reasons to support your answer.

4) Can you remember life before SNS? How has the way you communicate with people changed since then?

5) What things do you think are most important in a relationship? Be specific.

B Phrase Banks Review

Rephrase the underlined expressions and then rewrite the sentences.

1) Suggesting Options

- <u>Would this be okay?</u> How about discussing the first time we fell in love?

- I was thinking we could discuss the way we interact with others online. <u>Would this fit our criteria?</u>

2) Rejecting Options

- <u>I don't share your view on</u> social networking sites.

3) Asking to Reconsider

- <u>Why don't you think it over?</u> I think he had a good point about the internet alienating us.

- <u>Could you think further about that?</u> I think there are good reasons some people might prefer eating alone.

4) Looking for Assumptions

- <u>We are assuming that</u> people need to try to keep a soul-mate.

- <u>Is it really necessary that</u> we buy into cultural norms about whether or not it's okay to eat alone?

5) Accepting Options

- <u>That would work!</u> Making time to see friends offline is important.

- <u>That sounds quite convincing to me.</u> Trying to keep the passion alive in marriage is necessary for happiness.

6) Restating the Options

- <u>The advantage of this option is</u> that you can stay in contact with friends who live far away.

- <u>The disadvantage of this one is</u> it would require people to give up access to social networking services.

7) Offering a Similar Instance or Expression

- <u>In other words,</u> it's easy to fall out of love if you don't work at it.

8) Pointing Out Mistakes

- <u>I'm afraid it was off topic.</u> You shouldn't assume that everyone who eats alone is lonely.

Excellent! Now You are Ready to Go Onto the Next Topic!

LESSON 11

Global Warming:
Let's Love Our Earth!

- **Learning Objectives**
  After completing this lesson, you will be able to…

- Give logical opinions about global warming and actions to combat it.
- Utilize useful discussion phrases regarding prioritizing criteria and stating values.

1. Warming Up!

A *Check* the words you know and *circle* the words that you do not yet know.

Voca-space

temperature	intense	promising
greenhouse	extinction	wind power
solar power	reliable	replacement
energy source	biofuel	alternative
droughts	sustainable	efficiency
dwindling		

B In groups, help each other to find the meaning of the circled words. The dictionary should be the last resort!

2. Making a Case [A]

Read the article below. Gather ideas about the topic as you read the article.

Earth is Heating Up

In just one hundred years, Earth has gone from one of its coldest decades in thousands of years to one of its hottest. Scientists from the National Science Foundation report that, between 2000 and 2009, worldwide temperatures were hotter than they were in 75% of the last 11,300 years. **What is responsible for** the change? Many think the "**greenhouse effect**" is to blame. It happens when some gases in the Earth's atmosphere trap heat in, just like the walls of a **greenhouse**. It is what makes Earth warm enough to live on, but it is possible to get **too much of a good thing**.

Since the last ice age, Earth's **temperature** has **been fairly constant**. In the last century, this **started to change due to** large amounts of greenhouse gases produced by modern **human activities**, like burning fossil fuels. With amounts of greenhouse gases rising, Earth's temperature is rising as well.

Rising temperatures worldwide are **causing many new environmental problems**, like melting Earth's remaining ice sheets, raising sea levels, and causing extreme weather patterns. These changes lead to more **intense** storms, longer and drier **droughts**, the **extinction** of many plants and animals, and the loss of water supplies worldwide.

86 | Active Discussion 1

A Stretch Your Thinking

In groups, brainstorm ideas and opinions about the topic on the provided mind map. The provided keywords from [A] are to be used as starting points.

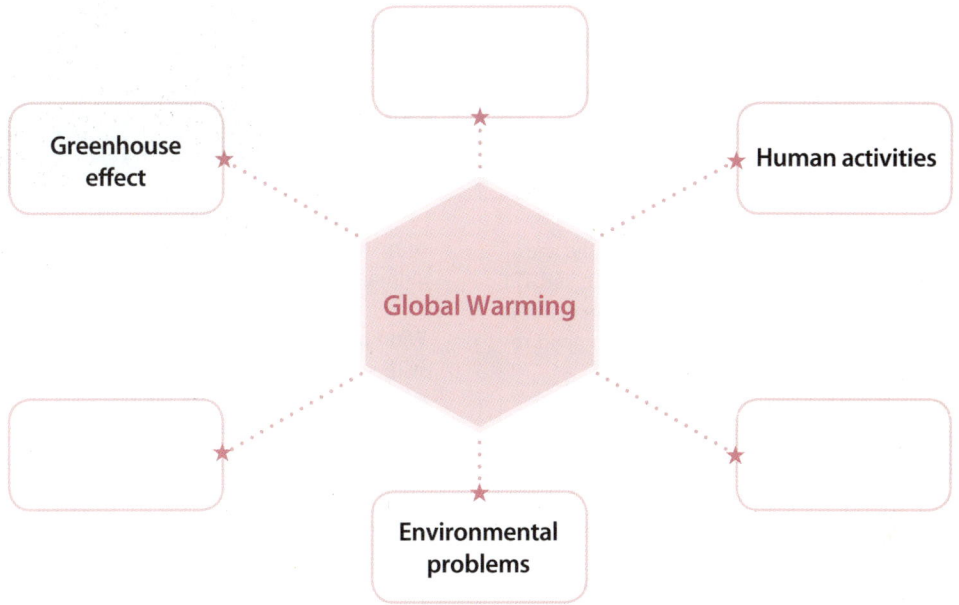

B Phrase Fit

greenhouse effect	too much of a good thing
been fairly constant	what is responsible for
started to change due to	causing many new environmental problems

Fill in the blanks using the above expressions to complete the sentences which are about [A].

1) In the last hundred years, Earth's temperature

   ....

   a large increase in greenhouse gases.

2) The ....
   occurs when certain atmospheric gases hold heat in, just like what happens in a greenhouse.

3) The greenhouse effect makes Earth warm enough for human life, but lately we are

   getting ....
   lately.

C True or False?

Circle TRUE if the statement corresponds with [A]; if not, circle FALSE.

1) The greenhouse effect decreases the temperature of Earth and is an environmental problem.
   (TRUE / FALSE)

2) The last decade was hotter than 20% of the last 11,300 years.   (TRUE / FALSE)

Correct and rewrite each false statement below.

....

....

....

....

....

Lesson 11 / Global Warming: Let's Love Our Earth!

2. Making a Case [B]

Read the article below. Gather ideas about the topic as you read the article.

The Bright Future of Alternative Energy

With Earth's oil supply **dwindling**, the age of fossil fuels is quickly coming to an end. Oil **is far from a** perfect **energy source**, but it is impossible to **quit cold turkey** without a good **replacement**.

Many organizations worldwide are currently researching alternative energy sources. They need to improve the **efficiency** of these sources, so that one day we can stop depending on oil. Although great improvements have been made, there are still some **kinks to be worked out** for three of the most **promis-ing** sources.

· **Solar Power** converts sunlight into electricity. All that is needed now is an efficient storage method to make it a **reliable** option when the sun is not shining.

· **Wind power** produces energy with windmills. As with solar power, storage is also an important issue for days when it is not windy.

· **Biofuels** are produced from living plants and animals. Although very promising, some experts worry that this may produce more greenhouse gas than actual fossil fuels.

Despite some issues, the future of alternative energy is bright. Many are confident that a **sustainable** replacement for fossil fuels is **just over the horizon.**

A Stretch Your Thinking

In groups, brainstorm ideas and opinions about the topic on the provided mind map. The provided keywords from [B] are to be used as starting points.

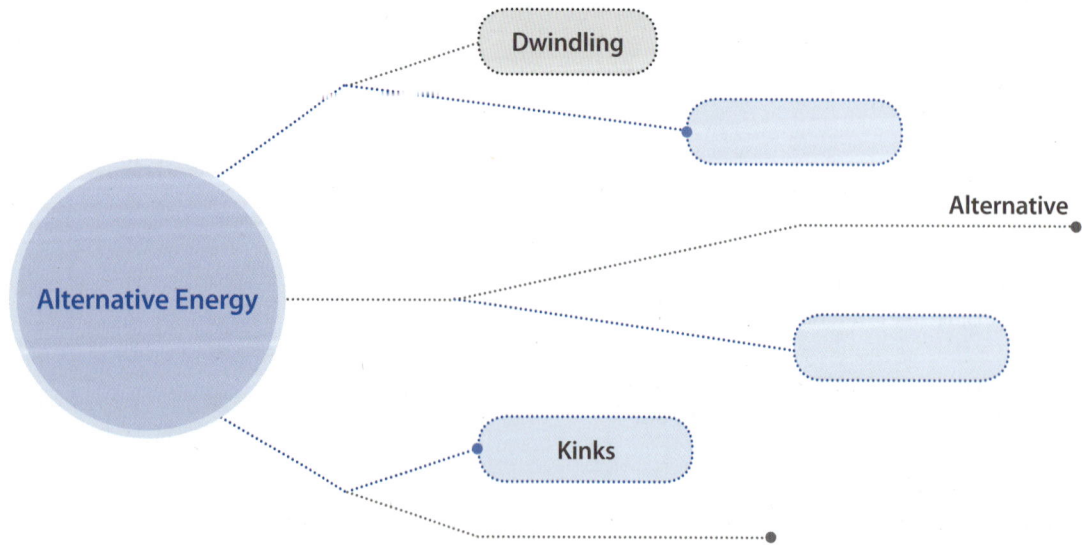

B Phrase Fit

is far from a	kinks to be worked out
quit cold turkey	just over the horizon
the future of alternative energy	despite some issues

Fill in the blanks using the above expressions to complete the sentences which are about [B].

1) At the moment, there are still some _____ with many alternatives to fossil fuels.

2) Many believe that a good replacement for fossil fuels is _____.

3) There are many problems with fossil fuels, but we cannot _____ until an alternative is found.

C True or False?

Circle TRUE if the statement corresponds with [B]; if not, circle FALSE.

1) The future of our Earth is bright, as scientists are currently working on alternative sources of energy that do not cause environmental problems. (TRUE / FALSE)

2) Biofuels are a great way to reduce greenhouse gas in the environment. (TRUE / FALSE)

Correct and rewrite each false statement below.

_____
_____
_____
_____

3. What's Your Opinion?

Share your opinions about the discussion questions below using the provided useful expressions from the Phrase Bank as much as possible.

1) Why is global warming a serious problem? Explain in detail.

2) What can we do to help stop global warming? Be specific.

3) Do you think the weather has changed since you were young? How so?

4) What kind of alternative energy sources would work in your country? Why? Give specific reasons.

5) Do you have suggestions or ideas about a possible alternative energy source? Be specific.

Phrase Bank

• **Prioritizing Criteria**
- [ ] What is more important to you, (A) or (B)?
- [ ] What do you value more?
- [ ] Which is the least important?
- [ ] How do you judge the worthiness of…?
- [ ] Which factor is most relevant?
- [ ] What aspect is most overlooked?
- [ ] Weighing the options, it seems….
- [ ] The pros and cons dictate….
- [ ] Every issue has plusses and minuses.

• **Stating Values**
- [ ] To me, (A) is more important than (B).
- [ ] To me, that doesn't matter.
- [ ] To me, that is really important.
- [ ] What we should really focus on is….
- [ ] Let's not get distracted by….
- [ ] It is easy to miss….
- [ ] In the long run, we should care most about….
- [ ] Over time, what will become apparent is….

4. Raise the Issues!

Pros & Cons

What's More Important: Being Comfortable Now or Saving Energy?

People need energy for many things every day. Scientists persistently try to work out the energy problems and it seems like a replacement to fossil fuel will be discovered very soon. Is it still necessary to try to reduce our energy usage? Should people just try to live comfortably without worrying about saving energy?

Are You Pros or Cons?   • Pro ☐   • Con ☐

A Make two groups: pros and cons. Come up with a supporting argument for your position on the given topic. Follow the reasoning method provided below.

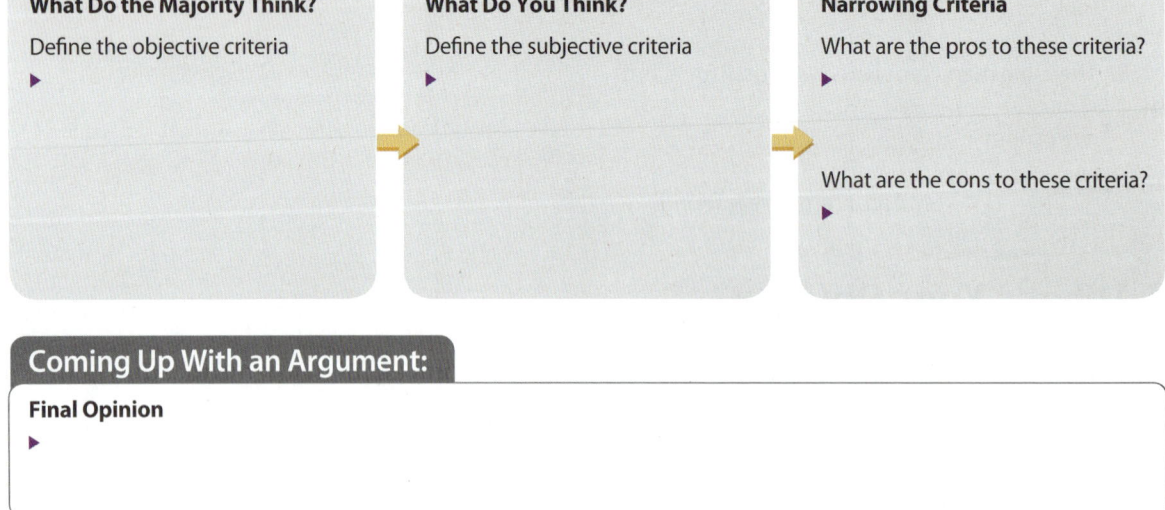

What Do the Majority Think?
Define the objective criteria
▸

What Do You Think?
Define the subjective criteria
▸

Narrowing Criteria
What are the pros to these criteria?
▸

What are the cons to these criteria?
▸

Coming Up With an Argument:

Final Opinion
▸

B Discuss your supporting ideas with the opposing group. All members of the group should participate in giving and answering the questions.

Phrase Bank

• Prioritizing Criteria
- ☐ What is more important to you, (A) or (B)?
- ☐ What do you value more?
- ☐ Which is the least important?
- ☐ How do you judge the worthiness of…?
- ☐ Which factor is most relevant?
- ☐ What aspect is most overlooked?
- ☐ Weighing the options, it seems….
- ☐ The pros and cons dictate….
- ☐ Every issue has plusses and minuses.

• Stating Values
- ☐ To me, (A) is more important than (B).
- ☐ To me, that doesn't matter.
- ☐ To me, that is really important.
- ☐ What we should really focus on is….
- ☐ Let's not get distracted by….
- ☐ It is easy to miss….
- ☐ In the long run, we should care most about….
- ☐ Over time, what will become apparent is….

5. Fun Forum

Q1 If you could omit ONE event in your life, what would it be? Why? Give specific reasons.

_____
_____
_____
_____

Q2 Now discuss with your group members about their choice of the one event in life they would like to erase. Are these events similar to yours? Are they different?

_____
_____
_____
_____

A Sneak Peek!

If you were a host to a Roundtable Discussion program, what would you ask about the following topic? Write three questions and discuss about it.

[Eating Local Food]

1.
2.
3.

Lesson 11 / Global Warming: Let's Love Our Earth!

12 ★ Culture Lab

Food Waste and Food Mileage

- **Learning Objectives**
  After completing this lesson, you will be able to…

- Give logical opinions about food waste and food mileage.
- Utilize useful discussion phrases regarding grasping the meaning of others' opinions and concluding a discussion.

1. Warming Up!

A *Check* the words you know and *circle* the words that you do not yet know.

Voca-space

transporting	habits	methane
public awareness	travels	consumer
globalization	kinder	estimated
developed countries	locally grown	disposal
food mileage	encourages	

B In groups, help each other to find the meaning of the circled words. The dictionary should be the last resort!

2. Making a Case [A]

Read the article below. Gather ideas about the topic as you read the article.

Wasteful Societies

Every year, around a third of food produced worldwide ends up in the trash. Combined, this **waste** is roughly 1.3 billion tons of food a year. **To put it another way**, consumers in **developed countries** waste an amount of food **nearly equal to** sub-Saharan Africa's net food production each year.

In countries like the United States, food waste is **estimated** to **cost as much as** $165 billion a year. Besides wasting money, this waste causes many environmental problems. It produces **methane**, a gas which causes global warming. In addition, transporting and producing food **uses up a lot of** resources like water and fuel.

To effectively reduce waste, it is necessary to increase awareness at a household level. For this reason, many countries are **trying to cut down** food waste through **public awareness** campaigns like the UK's "Love Food, Hate Waste" campaign. Some countries like South Korea are experimenting with **disposal** measures such as Radio Frequency Identification (RFID) waste disposal systems which charge citizens for the food they throw away by weight. **Through efforts such as** these, governments hope to shape their societies' **habits** to be less wasteful.

A Stretch Your Thinking

In groups, brainstorm ideas and opinions about the topic on the provided mind map. The provided keywords from [A] are to be used as starting points.

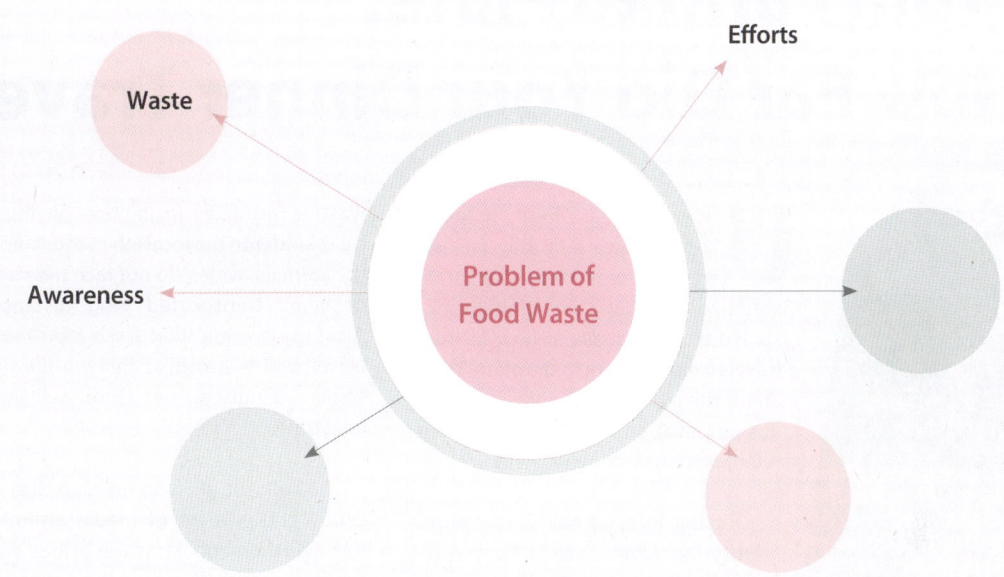

B Phrase Fit

to put it another way	nearly equal to
through efforts such as	trying to cut down
uses up a lot of	cost as much as

Fill in the blanks using the above expressions to complete the sentences which are about [A].

1) On a yearly basis, people living in developed countries waste an amount of food that is
_____ what the entire region of sub-Saharan Africa produces.

2) On top of wasting money, growing and bringing the food to customers far away,
_____ water and other resources.

3) _____ public awareness campaigns, governments hope to make their citizens more concerned about wasting food.

C True or False?

Circle TRUE if the statement corresponds with [A]; if not, circle FALSE.

1) Every year, people worldwide throw away a quarter of the food produced.
(TRUE / FALSE)

2) Food waste contributes to environmental problems like global warming.
(TRUE / FALSE)

Correct and rewrite each false statement below.

_____
_____
_____
_____

2. Making a Case [B]

Read the article below. Gather ideas about the topic as you read the article.

From Farm to Plate:
How Far Did Your Dinner Travel?

Understanding "**food mileage**" is being aware of how far food traveled to get to the **consumer**. Some people believe that **globalization** has led to an increase in how far food **travels** from the farm to the plate. Think about the labels at the supermarket—it's not uncommon to see "fresh" vegetables from continents away.

Buying local is **gaining in popularity** for many reasons. Supporters of the "food miles" concept **want to make people aware** of **the environmental impact of transporting** food over long distances, such as increasing greenhouse gases and wasting resources. In addition, buying local is **kinder** to the local job market and to the animals, which **do not face the stress of** being **transported long distances**. Also, some argue that fresh food tastes better and is healthier for you because some vitamins do not store well for a long time.

The concept of "food mileage" has recently gotten **a lot of media attention** through the support of celebrities such as Chef Jamie Oliver, who **encourages** people to buy local. The spread of the food mileage movement has caused an increase in farmers markets and restaurants offering "**locally grown**" menus.

A Stretch Your Thinking

In groups, brainstorm ideas and opinions about the topic on the provided mind map. The provided keywords from [B] are to be used as starting points.

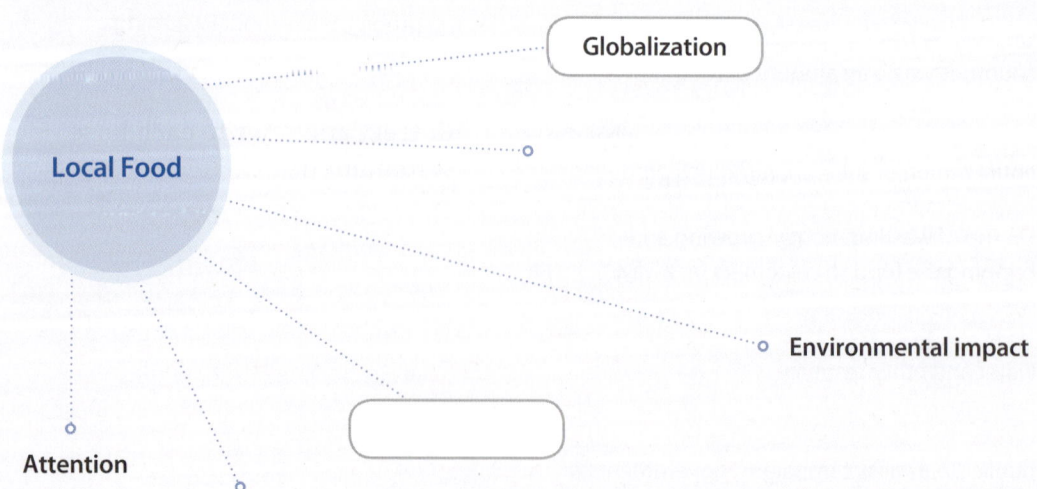

B Phrase Fit

gaining in popularity	do not face the stress of
a lot of media attention	want to make people aware
transported long distances	the environmental impact of

Fill in the blanks using the above expressions to complete the sentences which are about [B].

1) The food mileage movement, which involves buying locally produced food, is .... for a variety of reasons.

2) Supporters of the "food miles" concept want to increase awareness of .... transporting food across great distances, like wasting resources and increasing greenhouse gases.

3) The food mileage movement has recently gotten .... through the support of celebrities.

C True or False?

Circle TRUE if the statement corresponds with [B]; if not, circle FALSE.

1) Being aware of food mileage means knowing where your food came from.
(TRUE / FALSE)

2) Many people maintain that fresher food is more delicious and nutritious because the vitamins in fresh food do not store well.
(TRUE / FALSE)

Correct and rewrite each false statement below.

....
....
....
....
....

3. What's Your Opinion?

Share your opinions about the discussion questions below using the provided useful expressions from the Phrase Bank as much as possible.

1) List three ways we can reduce food waste. Be specific.

2) Do you usually worry about where food comes from? Why or why not? Give specific reasons.

3) List three ways to encourage people to buy local food. Be specific.

4) Are grocery stores and restaurants in your country required to post where ingredients come from? Do you think that this is necessary? Why or why not? Give specific reasons.

5) What are some problems associated with the food miles concept. Give specific reasons.

Phrase Bank

• **Grasping the Meaning**
- ☐ (Excuse me, but) what does (expression) mean?
- ☐ What do you mean by…?
- ☐ I'm sorry, but I didn't get what you said.
- ☐ If we draw a conclusion,….
- ☐ If we connect the dots, then….
- ☐ Putting two and two together, we can see that….

• **Concluding**
- ☐ In retrospect, this seems to….
- ☐ After considering all the main points,….
- ☐ Taking everything we've discussed into account,….
- ☐ On that note, we'll end by saying….
- ☐ All these points lead to….
- ☐ Thus, the overarching point is….
- ☐ In conclusion, the core point is….

Lesson 12 / Food Waste and Food Mileage

4. Raise the Issues!

Pros & Cons

What's a Better Way to Protect the Environment: Eating Local or Reducing Food Waste?

There are many ways we can improve the environment by changing our eating habits. Reducing food waste helps save money and reduce greenhouse gases. On the other hand, eating local food has benefits like saving resources that would have been wasted while transporting the food. To protect the environment, is eating local food a better way than reducing food waste?

Are You Pros or Cons? • Pro ☐   • Con ☐

A Make two groups: pros and cons. Come up with a supporting argument for your position on the given topic. Follow the reasoning method provided below.

What Do the Majority Think?	What Do You Think?	Narrowing Criteria
Define the objective criteria ▶	Define the subjective criteria ▶	What are the pros to these criteria? ▶ What are the cons to these criteria? ▶

Coming Up With an Argument:

Final Opinion
▶

B Discuss your supporting ideas with the opposing group. All members of the group should participate in giving and answering the questions.

Phrase Bank

• Grasping the Meaning
- ☐ (Excuse me, but) what does (expression) mean?
- ☐ What do you mean by…?
- ☐ I'm sorry, but I didn't get what you said.
- ☐ If we draw a conclusion,….
- ☐ If we connect the dots, then….
- ☐ Putting two and two together, we can see that….

• Concluding
- ☐ In retrospect, this seems to….
- ☐ After considering all the main points,….
- ☐ Taking everything we've discussed into account,….
- ☐ On that note, we'll end by saying….
- ☐ All these points lead to….
- ☐ Thus, the overarching point is….
- ☐ In conclusion, the core point is….

Active Discussion 1

5. Fun Forum

Food You Can't Live Without

Q1 If you had to choose only three foods and two drinks to eat for the rest of your life, what would they be? Give specific reasons for your choices.

Q2 Now discuss your chosen menu with your group members. Are they similar or different from yours? Looking at others' choices, would you change your mind regarding your chosen menu?

Issue 5: Our Earth

1 Word Power

The bold words provided are from the articles in this issue. Circle the synonyms and underline the antonyms.

• **dwindling**	Abating	Contracting	Ebbing	Subsiding	Swelling
• **sustainable**	Feasible	Illogical	Maintainable	Credible	Untenable
• **replacement**	Surrogate	Necessity	Alternative	Essential	Substitute
• **encourages**	Dampens	Rouses	Depresses	Dispirits	Dissuades
• **habits**	Conventions	Impulses	Urges	Predispositions	Inclinations
• **kinder**	Bitter	Inconsiderate	Sympathetic	Tender	Antagonistic

2 Thinking it Over

A Voice Your Opinion

Let's rethink about the discussion questions from the lessons of this issue. Consolidate your discussion skills while giving opinions to the discussion questions below.

1) What can we do to help stop global warming? Be specific.

2) Do you have suggestions or ideas about a possible alternative energy source? Be specific.

3) List three ways we can reduce food waste. Be specific.

4) Are grocery stores and restaurants in your country required to post where ingredients come from? Do you think that this is necessary? Why or why not? Give specific reasons.

5) What are some problems associated with the food miles concept? Give specific reasons to support your answer.

B Phrase Banks Review

Rephrase the underlined expressions and then rewrite the sentences.

1) Prioritizing Criteria

- **What is more important to you,** eating local **or** reducing food waste?

  ....

- **What do you value more?** Reducing global warming or enjoying modern conveniences like air-conditioning?

  ....

- **Weighing the options, it seems** that we should try to develop new alternative energy sources.

  ....

2) Stating Values

- **To me,** protecting the environment **is more important than** being able to buy certain kinds of seasonal produce year-round.

  ....

- **It is easy to miss** the effect that our eating habits have on the environment.

  ....

3) Grasping the Meaning

- **If we connect the dots, then** it is obvious that the environmental factors alone are a good reason to invest in alternative energy.

  ....

- **What do you mean by** "individual efforts are key"?

  ....

4) Concluding

- **In retrospect, this seems to** be the most logical solution to the food waste problem.

  ....

- **Taking everything we've discussed into account,** there is clear evidence to suggest that eating locally really is better for us.

  ....

- **Thus, the overarching point is** that individuals have a responsibility to consider the effect that their actions have on the environment.

  ....

Answer Key

Lesson 1
Is Stress Always Negative?

Case A: The Downside of Stress

Phrase Fit

1. on a daily basis.
2. contrary to popular belief
3. common problems associated with

True or False?

1. False:
   Model answer- Stress is not necessarily negative, but it can have negative effects when it goes unrelieved for too long.
2. True

Case B: The Upside of Stress

Phrase Fit

1. some research suggests
2. come into play
3. burst of energy

True or False?

1. True
2. False:
   Model answer- Some research suggests stress hormones can protect against diseases like Alzheimer's by stimulating brain function.

Lesson 2
Is Your Diet Working?

Case A: The Dieter's Dilemma

Phrase Fit

1. strictly adhering to
2. to a T
3. most importantly

True or False?

1. True
2. False:
   Model answer- Fad diets do not always work well, because they do not take into consideration your unique physiology and metabolism.

Case B: Eat and Exercise!

Phrase Fit

1. is the key to guaranteeing
2. the overall success of
3. on its own

True or False?

1. True
2. False:
   Model answer- Exercising daily is the key to long-term weight loss and physical health.

Active Discussion 1

Lesson 3 (Culture lab) Tanned vs White Skin, Which is More Beautiful?

Case A: White Skin: The Asian Ideal

Phrase Fit

1. shell out big cash
2. are putting out
3. with a hefty price tag

True or False?

1. False:
   Model answer- By removing pigments like melanin from the skin, whitening treatments reduce your body's natural protection against the sun's rays.
2. True

Case B: Baking for Beauty: Tanning in Western Countries

Phrase Fit

1. went to great lengths to
2. gained popularity among
3. however you accomplish it

True or False?

1. False:
   Model answer- Tanning was a popularly prescribed treatment in the past, but now there is a lot of negative publicity about UV rays increasing the risk of skin cancer.
2. True

Issue 1 Beauty and Health: Wrap Up

Word Power

- **Perception:**
  - **Synonym-** Recognition, Awareness, Appraisal, Understanding
  - **Antonym-** Misunderstanding

- **Stimulating:**
  - **Synonym-** Invigorating, Electrifying, Provocative
  - **Antonym-** Debilitating, Exhausting

- **Consistency:**
  - **Synonym-** Accord, Cohesion, Regularity
  - **Antonym-** Variation, Nonconformity

- **Accountable:**
  - **Synonym-** Obligated, Liable
  - **Antonym-** Untrustworthy, Blameless, Irresponsible

- **Epitome:**
  - **Synonym-** Archetype, Embodiment, Essence, Manifestation
  - **Antonym-** Misrepresentation

- **Quintessential:**
  - **Synonym-** Principal, Primary, Definitive
  - **Antonym-** Secondary, Minor

Phrase Banks Review Model Answers

1. Changing the Subject

- <u>From now on, let's focus on</u> a discussion about the risks of sun tanning.

- I think to get a fuller understanding we should also explore crash dieting.

2. **Cancelling Prior Ideas**
   - What I meant to say was that tanned skin is usually more beautiful to me.

3. **Taking a Position**
   - My position is that exercising is necessary to build a healthy body.
   - Looking at all the options, it is best to share some of our own favorite diet tips.

4. **Checking Another's Opinion**
   - What's your feeling on the issue of fad diets?
   - What's your take on effective ways to relieve stress?

5. **Clarifying a Position**
   - Well, I think the answer is that some people have trouble losing weight no matter what they do.

6. **Confirming a Position**
   - You mentioned to me that stress has negative side effects; is that right?

7. **Resolving Misunderstandings**
   - I didn't quite mean it that way. Do you mean whiter skin looks cleaner than tanned skin?
   - I'm sorry. I think you misunderstood. I do think that stressful jobs should be avoided.

Lesson 4
Perfumes and Why We Love Them

Case A: Perfumes and Increased Sexual Attraction?

Phrase Fit
1. thought to stimulate
2. less pronounced; been known to produce
3. most scientists believe

True or False?
1. True
2. False:
   Model answer- Most scientists believe that the impact of pheromones on human behavior has decreased over the years due to advancements in modern society.

Case B: Pleasing Scents and Self-Identification

Phrase Fit
1. will literally become
2. can recall
3. truly important

True or False?
1. True
2. True

Lesson 5 (Culture lab)
Fermented Food: Cheese or Fermented Soybeans?

Case A: The Spread of Cheese Culture

Phrase Fit
1. shrouded in mystery
2. a key ingredient in

3 is believed to have been

True or False?

1 False:
   Model answer- No one knows who discovered the first cheese, but legend has it that nomads stumbled upon the process by accident.

2 True

Case B: Indigenous Asian Cuisine, Fermented Soybeans

Phrase Fit

1 in many forms
2 an essential part of
3 relatively unknown outside of

True or False?

1 True
2 False:
   Model answer- Fermented soybean paste has many health benefits, including providing essential vitamins, minerals, and linoleic acid, extending longevity, and reducing body fat.

Issue 2 Daily Lives: Wrap Up

Word Power

- **Civilized:**
  Synonyms- Enlightened, Advanced, Knowledgeable, Accomplished
  Antonyms- Inexperienced

- **Combine:**
  Synonyms- Associate, Merge Link
  Antonyms- Separate, Disconnect

- **Desire:**
  Synonyms- Ambition, Longing, Rapture
  Antonyms- Aversion, Indifference

- **Essential:**
  Synonyms- Fundamental, Vital, Indispensible
  Antonyms- Secondary, Auxiliary

- **Serendipitously:**
  Synonyms- Unintentionally, Spontaneously, Accidentally
  Antonyms- Deliberately, Painstakingly

- **Purported:**
  Synonyms- Alleged, Implied, Apparent
  Antonyms- True, Actual

Phrase Banks Review Model Answers

1. Introducing Your Experience

- One of my worst experiences was when I tried some really pungent Dutch cheese.
- I remember when I went to a shop where you could mix your own fragrances. It was amazing.

2. Beginning the Discussion

- Let's discuss our experiences trying different fermented foods.
- It's a good idea to begin with discussing our first experiences purchasing perfume.

3. Contributing Ideas

- To reach our goal, we could try each sharing some of our favorite memories about perfume.

- What about this—sharing some of the things you look for in a new perfume?

4. Encouraging Ideas

- I like that! I agree with your point about perfumes changing with people's personal scents.
- Awesome! I never thought that fermented tofu could taste this great!

5. Expanding on Ideas

- That gives me an idea. Let's share our personal opinions about different fermented foods.
- Another idea would be to discuss how we pick fragrances for different occasions.

Lesson 6
Food Crisis

Case A: The Global Food Crisis

Phrase Fit

1. causes a variety of
2. in recent years
3. be surprised to learn that

True or False?

1. False:
   Model answer- In recent years, the problem has gotten worse due to rising food prices and the spread of the global recession.
2. True

Case B: A Need for Global Effort to Combat Famine

Phrase Fit

1. must band together
2. other actions that boost
3. growing concerns that famine

True or False?

1. True
2. True

Lesson 7 (Culture lab)
Beautiful Comradeships

Case A: Donating Life

Phrase Fit

1. have the option to choose
2. shortage of organs for transplantation
3. to become common practice

True or False?

1. False:
   Model answer- A much higher percentage of people usually participate in the opt-out programs.
2. True

Case B: Culture of Organ Donations

Phrase Fit

1. despite the benefits
2. can make it difficult for
3. the most common reasons for

True or False?

1. True
2. False:
   Model answer- This reason was not mentioned in the article.

Issue 3 Ethics: Wrap Up

Word Power

- **Substantial:**
  - **Synonyms-** Momentous, Considerable, Generous
  - **Antonyms-** Insignificant, Miniscule
- **Urgent:**
  - **Synonyms-** Pressing, Driving, Compelling, Critical
  - **Antonyms-** Irrelevant
- **Tackle:**
  - **Synonyms-** Endeavor, Strive, Venture
  - **Antonyms-** Neglect, Ignore
- **Invaluable:**
  - **Synonyms-** Instrumental, Significant
  - **Antonyms-** Unconstructive, Disadvantageous, Adverse
- **Reluctance:**
  - **Synonyms-** Hesitancy, Qualm, Hostility, Repulsion
  - **Antonyms-** Enthusiasm
- **Reliable:**
  - **Synonyms-** Conscientious, Unequivocal, Unimpeachable
  - **Antonyms-** Deceptive, Rash

Phrase Banks Review
Model Answers

1. Interrupting

- <u>Excuse me for interrupting, but</u> I don't think the hunger problem will be that easily solved.

2. Disagreeing with Positions

- <u>That might be true, but</u> try to see the issue from the side of people who need organs.
- <u>A lot of people might agree with that, but</u> there is no evidence to support that claim.

3. Defending Positions

- <u>I think the point I'm trying to make here is</u> I think all people should be required to donate their organs after death.
- <u>Well, if you could just spare me a moment,</u> I think if countries worldwide work together, we will be able to find a way to tackle the hunger crisis.

4. Agreeing with Positions

- <u>I think that's a good point.</u> Our society should consider the hunger problems of other nations before wasting food.
- <u>Absolutely.</u> Organ donation is like giving a gift to someone in need.
- <u>Certainly.</u> I agree that a collective effort is necessary to help those suffering from hunger.

Lesson 8
Expiration Date on Love?

Case A: The Science of Love

Phrase Fit

1. an urgency to
2. head-over-heels in love
3. over the course of

True or False?

1. False:
   Model answer- Although NGF decreases over time, but the bonding that occurs in this stage creates a good foundation for the mature relationship to continue on.
2. False:
   Model answer- High NGF levels come from a rush of adrenalin.

Case B: Forever and Always: How-To's on Keeping a Soul-mate Relationship

Phrase Fit

1. if you need it
2. can lead to
3. things that I have learned

True or False?

1. False:
   Model answer- The writer says not to value your children over your marital relationship.
2. True

Lesson 9
Cyber Relationships

Case A: Online Connections

Phrase Fit

1. since its creation
2. giving them a better chance of
3. maintaining relationships with

True or False?

1. False:
   Model answer- Social networking sites can help you interact with people all over the world.
2. True

Case B: Missing Out on Real Relationships

Phrase Fit

1. it may seem like you are
2. have a wide range of
3. keep a healthy balance between

True or False?

1. True
2. False:
   Model answer- SNS can never completely replace real-life connections and interactions with others.

Lesson 10 (Culture lab)
Collectivism and Individualism in Dining

Case A: Eating Alone is Embarassing?

Phrase Fit

1. a few sideways glances
2. a chance for bonding
3. might not just be

True or False?

1. False:
   Model answer- For people living in collectivist societies, sharing food is a communal activity, and in many situations, eating alone might not just be embarrassing, but also difficult.
2. True

Case B: Tips for Solo Diners

Phrase Fit

1. easier to find space
2. more embarrassment than
3. staring off into space

True or False?

1. False:
   Model answer- Recently, many restaurants have been cashing in on the trend of solo dining by offering single seats.
2. True

Issue 4 Social Lives: Wrap Up

Word Power

- **Vigor:**
  Synonyms- Endurance, Vehemence, Vitality
  Antonyms- Idleness, Lethargy
- **Elude:**
  Synonyms- Avoid, Outwit, Shirk
  Antonyms- Entice, Attract
- **Voyeuristic:**
  Synonyms- Curious, Peeping, Inquisitive
  Antonyms- Disinterested, Indifferent
- **Isolated:**
  Synonyms- Deserted, Sequestered, Withdrawn, Stranded
  Antonyms- Incorporated
- **Stigma:**
  Synonyms- Disgrace, Blemish
  Antonyms- Credit, Pride, Honor
- **Communal:**
  Synonyms- Collective, United
  Antonyms- Detached, Single, Individualistic

Phrase Banks Review
Model Answers

1. Suggesting Options

- <u>What if we did this?</u> How about discussing the first time we fell in love?
- I was thinking we could discuss the way we interact with others online. <u>Would this work?</u>

2. Rejecting Options

- <u>We don't see eye to eye on</u> social networking sites.

3. Asking to Reconsider

- <u>Please reconsider.</u> I think he had a good point about the internet alienating us.
- <u>Don't jump to conclusions.</u> I think there are good reasons some people might prefer eating alone.

4. Looking for Assumptions

- <u>What would happen if we</u> assume that people need to try to keep a soul-mate?
- <u>Do we really have to</u> buy into cultural norms about whether or not it's okay to eat alone?

5. Accepting Options

- That's a possibility! Making time to see friends offline is important.
- It sounds right to say that trying to keep the passion alive in marriage is necessary for happiness.

6. Restating the Options

- To emphasize what has been said so far, being able to stay in contact with friends who live far away is an advantage.
- To expand upon the points made so far, one of the disadvantages is that it would require people to give up access to social networking services.

7. Offering a Similar Instance or Expression

- That is to say it's easy to fall out of love if you don't work at it.

8. Pointing Out Mistakes

- I don't think you have it quite right. You shouldn't assume that everyone who eats alone is lonely.

Lesson 11
Global Warming: Let's Love Our Earth!

Case A: Earth is Heating Up

Phrase Fit

1. started to change due to
2. greenhouse effect
3. too much of a good thing

True or False?

1. False:
   Model answer- The greenhouse effect increases the temperature of Earth and is an environmental problem.
2. False:
   Model answer- The last decade was hotter than 75% of the last 11,300 years.

Case B: The Bright Future of Alternative Energy

Phrase Fit

1. kinks to be worked out
2. just over the horizon
3. quit cold turkey

True or False?

1. True
2. False:
   Model answer- Some experts think that biofuels might produce more greenhouse gas than fossil fuels.

Lesson 12 (Culture lab)
Food Waste and Food Mileage

Case A: Wasteful Societies

Phrase Fit

1. nearly equal to
2. uses up a lot of
3. through efforts such as

True or False?

1. False:
   Model answer- Every year, about a third of food produced worldwide gets thrown away.

2. True

Case B: From Farm to Plate: How Far Did Your Dinner Travel?

Phrase Fit

1. gaining in popularity
2. the environmental impact of
3. a lot of media attention

True or False?

1. True
2. False:
   Model answer- Many people maintain that fresher food is more delicious and nutritious because the vitamins store well in fresh food.

Issue 5 Our Earth: Wrap Up

Word Power

- **Dwindling:**

  Synonyms- Abating, Contracting, Ebbing, Subsiding

  Antonyms- Swelling

- **Sustainable:**

  Synonyms- Feasible, Maintainable, Credible

  Antonyms- Illogical, Untenable

- **Replacement:**

  Synonyms- Surrogate, Alternative, Substitute

  Antonyms- Necessity, Essential

- **Encourages:**

  Synonyms- Rouses

  Antonyms- Dampens, Depresses, Dispirits, Dissuades

- **Habits:**

  Synonyms- Conventions, Predispositions, Inclinations

  Antonyms- Impulses, Urges

- **Kinder:**

  Synonyms- Sympathetic, Tender

  Antonyms- Bitter, Inconsiderate, Antagonistic

Phrase Banks Review Model Answers

1. Prioritizing Criteria

- <u>Which factor is most relevant?</u> Eating local or reducing food waste?
- <u>What aspect is most overlooked?</u> Reducing global warming or enjoying modern conveniences like air-conditioning?
- <u>The pros and cons dictate</u> that we should try to develop new alternative energy sources.

2. Stating Values

- <u>What we should really focus on is</u> protecting the environment. It's more important than being able to buy certain kinds of seasonal produce year-round.
- <u>In the long run, we should care most about</u> the effect that our eating habits have on the environment.

3. Grasping the Meaning

- <u>Putting two and two together, we can see that</u> the environmental factors alone are a good reason to invest in alternative energy.

- <u>I'm sorry, but I didn't get what you said.</u> What does "individual efforts are key" mean?

4. Concluding

- <u>After considering all the main points,</u> I feel this might be the most logical solution to the food waste problem.

- <u>On that note, we'll end by saying</u> there is clear evidence to suggest that eating locally really is better for us.

- <u>In conclusion, the core point is</u> that individuals have a responsibility to consider the effect that their actions have the environment.